100 Word Puzzles on the Bible

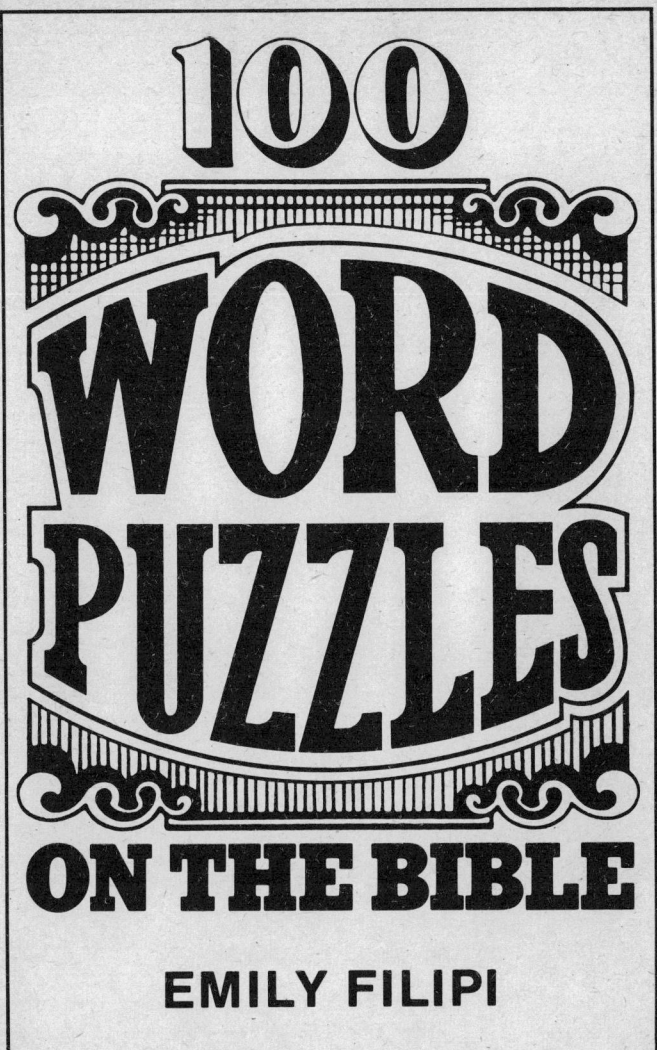

100 WORD PUZZLES ON THE BIBLE

EMILY FILIPI

Broadman Press
Nashville, Tennessee

© Copyright 1982 • Broadman Press

All rights reserved.

4291-07

ISBN: 0-8054-9107-4

Dewey Decimal Classification: 220

Subject Heading: BIBLE—QUESTION BOOKS

Library of Congress Catalog Card Number: 81-68367

Printed in the United States of America

To
Jane Hudson
a dear friend, loving critic,
prejudiced supporter, and
prayerful partner

1
Alike

The following people shared something alike. Match the persons with the thing they had alike.

1. Nebuchadnezzar and Aaron
   Daniel 3:1; Exodus 32:4
2. Jesus and Jonah
   Matthew 8:26; Jonah 1:15
3. Miriam and Naaman
   Numbers 12:10; 2 Kings 5:27
4. Daniel and Joseph
   Daniel 2:25 *ff.*; Genesis 41:25 *ff.*
5. Joseph and Zechariah
   Matthew 1:20; Luke 1:13
6. John the Baptist and Paul
   Mark 6:18; Acts 25:26
7. Jesus and Joseph
   Matthew 27:9; Genesis 37:28
8. Naboth and Jesus
   1 Kings 21:9-10; Mark 14:56
9. Judas and Joab
   Mark 14:44-45; 2 Samuel 20:9-10
10. Jesus and Micaiah
    Matthew 26:67; 1 Kings 22:24
11. Joseph and prodigal son
    Genesis 44:27-28; Luke 15:20

a. witnessed to kings
b. longed for by father
c. received a slap
d. built golden images
e. had leprosy
f. gave death kiss
g. stopped a storm
h. angels told of birth of a son
i. interpreted dreams
j. accused by false witnesses
k. sold for silver

2
Animals

Animals play an important role in the life of humanity. Match each statement with the correct animal.

1. Egypt was plagued with this amphibian
2. Spoke to its rider
3. Carried away sins on Day of Atonement
4. Licked the sores of Lazarus
5. Samson killed one with his hands
6. A pharaoh dreamed of fourteen
7. Transported Isaac's bride
8. Sacrificed as an offering by Abraham
9. Cannot change its spots
10. Tended by David for his father

a. kine, Genesis 41:18
b. sheep, 1 Samuel 17:34
c. ram, Genesis 22:13
d. lion, Judges 14:5-6
e. camel, Genesis 24:64
f. dogs, Luke 16:21
g. leopard, Jeremiah 13:23
h. frog, Exodus 8:6
i. goat, Leviticus 16:21
j. ass, Numbers 22:30

3
Assassinations

Each of these people were assassinated. Match the killer(s) with the victim.

1. Joab, 2 Samuel 18:14
2. Cain, Genesis 4:8
3. Herod, Matthew 14:6-10
4. Jehu, 2 Kings 9:30-33
5. Jael, Judges 4:21-22
6. Pekah, 2 Kings 15:23-25
7. Jehoiada, 2 Kings 11:15-16
8. Jozacar and Jehozabad, 2 Kings 12:20-21
9. Menahem, 2 Kings 15:14

a. John the Baptist
b. Abel
c. Pekahiah
d. Jezebel
e. Absalom
f. Sisera
g. Shallum
h. Athaliah
i. Joash

4
Associations

Match the person with the item associated with him or her.

1. Pottage
2. Plumbline
3. Harp
4. Ark
5. Axe head
6. Burning bush
7. Rib
8. Salt
9. Big fish
10. Frogs
11. Crumbs

a. Elisha, 2 Kings 6:1-6
b. Lazarus, Luke 16:20-21
c. Lot's wife, Genesis 19:26
d. Esau, Genesis 25:30
e. Moses, Exodus 3:3-4
f. Pharaoh, Exodus 8:2,6
g. Amos, Amos 7:7-8
h. Noah, Genesis 6:14
i. David, 1 Samuel 16:23
j. Jonah, Jonah 1:17
k. Eve, Genesis 2:21-22

5
Belongings

Match each of the following people with his or her belonging.

1. Joseph, Genesis 44:2
2. Jesus, John 19:23
3. Mary, John 12:3
4. Abraham, Genesis 22:6
5. Prodigal son, Luke 15:22
6. Solomon, 1 Kings 10:21
7. Jonathan, 1 Samuel 18:4
8. David, 1 Samuel 21:8-9
9. Paul, 2 Timothy 4:13
10. Dorcas, Acts 9:39

a. Spikenard
b. Silver cup
c. Seamless coat
d. Ring
e. Knife
f. Gold drinking vessel
g. Handmade coats
h. Cloak, books, and parchments
i. Sword, bow, and girdle
j. Goliath's sword

6
The Birth of Jesus

Each of the following people or groups had something to do with the story of the birth of Jesus. Match the people with the statement concerning them.

1. Caesar Augustus, Luke 2:1
2. Joseph, Luke 2:4
3. Mary, Luke 2:5
4. Angel, Luke 2:8-11
5. Shepherds, Luke 2:17
6. Those who heard, Luke 2:18
7. Herod, Matthew 2:7-8
8. Heavenly host, Luke 2:13-14
9. Wise Men, Matthew 2:11
10. God, Matthew 2:12

a. went to see Jesus, then told others about him
b. announced Jesus' birth to shepherds
c. issued a decree
d. went with her husband to Bethlehem
e. went to Bethlehem to be taxed
f. wondered at what they were told
g. said "glory to God in the highest"
h. presented gifts of gold, frankincense, and myrrh
i. warned the Wise Men of Herod's evil plan
j. pretended to want to worship Jesus

7
Bodies of Water

Water is a major source of recreation for many people today. It is also necessary for human beings to live. Match the bodies of water with the proper statement about water:

1. A blind man washed in this pool and received sight, John 9:6-7.
2. Naaman "dipped" in this river and was healed of leprosy, 2 Kings 5:14.
3. Daniel saw a vision of a ram in this river, Daniel 8:2-3.
4. Ezekiel saw visions of God here, Ezekiel 1:3.
5. Elijah slew the prophets of Baal near this brook, 1 Kings 18:40.
6. Moses led the Israelites through dry land at this sea, Exodus 14:16.
7. Another name for the Sea of Galilee, John 6:1.
8. A river which flows out of Eden, Genesis 2:10-11.
9. The water at this place was bitter, Exodus 15:23.
10. Seraiah was commanded to read a book and cast it into this river, Jeremiah 51:60-63.
11. Jesus taught in a ship in this body of water, Luke 5:1-3.

a. Marah
b. Gennesaret
c. Kishon
d. Tiberias
e. Euphrates
f. Pison
g. Red
h. Siloam
i. Chebar
j. Jordan
k. Ulai

8
Bows and Arrows

Fill in each blank with the person associated with bows and arrows.

1. _____ was an archer, Genesis 16:15; 21:20.
2. _____ was wounded by archers, and he asked his armourbearer to kill him with a sword, 1 Samuel 31:3-4.
3. _____ shot an arrow to warn David to flee from Saul, 1 Samuel 20:33-42.
4. _____ was hit by an arrow shot at random, and the king died, 1 Kings 22:34.
5. _____ was hit by archers and died in Jerusalem, 2 Chronicles 35:23-24.
6. _____ likened his condition to being compassed round about by archers, Job 16:13.
7. _____ was angry when Joash struck the ground only three times with an arrow, 2 Kings 13:17-19.
8. _____ prophecied that the king of Assyria would not shoot an arrow in Jerusalem, Isaiah 37:33.
9. _____ lamented over Saul and Jonathan and taught the children of Judah to use the bow, 2 Samuel 1:17-18.
10. _____ sent his son with his bow to get venison, Genesis 27:1-3.
11. _____ reminded the people assembled at Shechem that hornets, not bows, had defeated their enemies, Joshua 24:2,12.

9
Chariots

Chariots were often used in biblical days. Fill in each blank with the proper words which refer to each chariot experience.

1. The Ethiopian eunuch was reading _____ as he traveled between Jerusalem and Gaza, Acts 8:27-28.
2. Pharaoh used all the chariots of Egypt to chase the _____, Exodus 14:6-8.
3. _____ saw a chariot of fire before being taken to heaven by a whirlwind, 2 Kings 2:11.
4. God commanded _____ to cripple the horses and burn the chariots of King Jabin of Hazor, Joshua 11:1,6.
5. Pharaoh gave his ring to _____ and made him ride in Pharaoh's second chariot, Genesis 41:41-43.
6. In a war with Israel, the _____ had thirty thousand chariots and six thousand horsemen, 1 Samuel 13:5.
7. When he saw the sword of Barak, _____ got out of his chariot and fled on foot, Judges 4:14-15.
8. Elah, king of Judah, was killed by _____, the captain of half of the king's chariots, 1 Kings 16:8-10.
9. Isaiah rebuked _____ for taking pride in the multitude of his chariots, Isaiah 37:21-24.
10. After he was healed, _____ got out of his chariot when he saw Elisha's servant following him, 2 Kings 5:21.
11. _____ told Solomon that God said to use gold for the pattern of the chariot of the cherubims that spread their wings over the ark of the covenant, 1 Chronicles 28:18-19.

10
Children

Match each child with something connected to his childhood.

1. Moses, Exodus 2:3
2. Jesus, Luke 2:7
3. Jacob, Genesis 25:26
4. David, 1 Samuel 17:39-40
5. Joseph, Genesis 37:3
6. Samuel, 1 Samuel 2:18
7. Isaac, Genesis 22:6-13
8. Shunammite's son, 2 Kings 4:35-36
9. John (the Baptist), Luke 1:60-61
10. Esau, Genesis 25:25

a. sacrifice
b. seven sneezes
c. red hair
d. not a family name
e. ark (basket)
f. heel
g. coat of many colors
h. linen ephod
i. sling shot
j. manger

11
Christian Missions

Some of the most thrilling reading for the Christian is the story of the spread of the early church. Fill in each blank with the person or persons responsible for the mission effort.

1. _____ prayed with John that the Samaritans would receive the Holy Spirit, Acts 8:14-15.
2. _____ was sent by God to restore Saul's eye sight, Acts 9:10-12.
3. _____ witnessed to a eunuch in a chariot, Acts 8:26-27.
4. _____ sent Peter to Samaria to check on Philip's work, Acts 8:14.
5. _____ was stoned to death for his faith in Jesus, Acts 7:59.
6. _____ was the prophet the Ethiopian eunuch was reading, Acts 8:30.
7. _____ interceded in behalf of Saul after his conversion, Acts 9:27.
8. _____ caught Philip up, and the eunuch saw him no more, Acts 8:39.
9. _____ was blinded by a light on his way to persecute the Christians, Acts 9:1-3.
10. _____ wanted to buy the power of the Holy Spirit, Acts 8:18-19.

12
The Christmas Story

Fill in each blank with the correct answer about the Christmas story.

1. _____ was the home of Mary and Joseph, Luke 2:4.
2. _____ announced Jesus' birth to Mary, Luke 1:26-27.
3. _____ was the town where Jesus was born, Luke 2:4-7.
4. _____ was where Jesus was laid, Luke 2:7.
5. _____ in a manger was the sign the shepherds were to look for to find Jesus, Luke 2:12.
6. _____ kept the sayings of the shepherds in her heart, Luke 2:19.
7. _____ guided the Wise Men to Jesus, Matthew 2:2.
8. _____ was where the Wise Men found Jesus, Matthew 2:11.
9. _____ warned the Wise Men of Herod's trick, Matthew 2:12.
10. _____ told Joseph to flee with Jesus to Egypt, Matthew 2:13.

13
Creatures

The creatures God made were often used to teach important lessons. Fill in the blanks with the name of the proper creature.

1. Jesus cautioned people not to "cast ye your pearls before _____, lest they trample them under their feet," Matthew 7:6.
2. The writer of Proverbs tells us, "Go to the _____, thou sluggard; consider her ways, and be wise," Proverbs 6:6.
3. God used the foolishness of an _____ which lays her eggs on the earth where they may be stepped on to convince Job of God's mighty works, Job 39:13-17.
4. Jesus illustrated God's care for mankind by these words, "Are not two _____ sold for a farthing? and one of them shall not fall on the ground without your Father," Matthew 10:29.
5. Jesus likened his love for Jerusalem to a _____ which gathered her little ones under her wing, Matthew 23:37.
6. Isaiah likened the person who waited upon the Lord to _____ which soar above the earth, Isaiah 40:31.
7. The psalmist used the "_____ upon a thousand hills" to show God's ownership of everything, Psalm 50:10.
8. The psalmist advised, "Be ye not as the _____, . . . which have no understanding: whose mouth must be held in with bit," Psalm 32:9.
9. Luke described Jesus as being "led as a _____ to the slaughter," Acts 8:32.
10. Solomon said, "The righteous are bold as a _____," Proverbs 28:1.

14
Denials

The following people each denied something. Match the person with what he or she denied.

1. Abraham, Genesis 20:2
2. Peter, Matthew 26:69-70
3. Jonathan, 1 Samuel 20:9
4. Adam, Genesis 3:12
5. Job, Job 13:14-18
6. Sarah, Genesis 18:15
7. The crowd around Jesus, Luke 8:45
8. Barnabas, Acts 14:12-15
9. Pilate, Luke 23:4
10. Chief priests, John 19:21
11. Eliphaz, Job 4:1,7

a. That the innocent perish
b. That he was a god
c. That Jesus was guilty
d. That Jesus was the King of the Jews
e. That he would not tell David of his father's intentions
f. That his wife was his wife
g. That he was being punished for sin
h. That she laughed at an angel's message
i. That he was responsible for eating the forbidden fruit
j. That anyone had touched Jesus
k. That he knew Jesus

15
Depression

Fill in the blanks with the names of the people who experienced depression.

_____ 1. "If thou deal thus with me, kill me, I pray thee, out of hand, if I have found favour in thy sight; and let me not see my retchedness."

_____ 2. "Therefore now, O Lord, take, I beseech thee, my life from me; for it is better for me to die than to live."

_____ 3. "But he himself went a day's journey into the wilderness, and came and sat down under a juniper tree: and he requested for himself that he might die; and said, It is enough; now, O Lord, take away my life; for I am not better than my fathers."

_____ 4. "Then said I, Woe is me! for I am undone; because I am a man of unclean lips, and I dwell in the midst of a people of unclean lips: for mine eyes have seen the King, Lord of hosts."

_____ 5. "I am sore distressed; for the Philistines make war against me, and God is departed from me, and answereth me no more, neither by prophets, nor by dreams."

_____ 6. "When (he) perceived all that was done, (he) rent his clothes, and put on sackcloth with ashes, and went out into the midst of the city, and cried with a loud and bitter cry."

_____ 7. "They say unto her, Woman, why weepest thou? She saith unto them, Because they have taken away my Lord, and I know not where they have laid him."

In most of these cases of depression, and others in the Bible, the depression was overcome by service to God. For example, Jeremiah felt he had been deceived by God and vowed never to speak God's name again (Jer. 20:7-9). But in verses 12 and 13, Jeremiah spoke of his problem to the Lord and continued to serve the Lord.

16
Desires

Every individual has desires he would like to see fulfilled. Match the person with his desire:

1. Certain Greeks, John 12:21
2. Bartimaeus, Mark 10:46,51
3. Paul, Romans 10:1
4. Mother of John and James, Matthew 20:21
5. Pilate, Matthew 27:24
6. Hannah, 1 Samuel 1:9-11
7. Lazarus, Luke 16:21
8. Solomon, 2 Chronicles 1:7-12
9. Esther, Esther 7:3
10. Daniel, Daniel 1:8
11. Eunuch, Acts 8:30-31

a. to understand the Scriptures
b. Crumbs from a table
c. save her people
d. sight
e. see Jesus
f. wisdom and knowledge
g. salvation of Israel
h. to eat food of his choosing
i. innocence of Jesus' blood
j. right and left seats for sons
k. a child

17
The Disciples

Fill in each blank with the name of one of the twelve disciples whom Jesus chose to help him in his ministry.

1. _____ and _____ were good friends, John 1:45.
2. _____ was a tax collector before becoming a disciple, Matthew 9:9.
3. _____, _____, _____, and _____ left their jobs as fishermen to become disciples, Matthew 4:18-21.
4. _____ betrayed Jesus, Matthew 27:3.
5. The son of Alphaeus was _____, Matthew 10:3.
6. The disciple Lebbaeus was also known as _____, Matthew 10:3.
7. _____ wanted to see the nail prints in the hands of Jesus, John 20:24-25.
8. The name used to differentiate between Simon Peter and the other Simon was _____, Mark 3:18.
9. _____ took the place of Judas after Jesus ascended into heaven, Acts 1:26.

18
Doves

Answer each of the following questions concerning doves.

_____ 1. Who sent a dove to see if the water had dried off the earth, Genesis 8:6-8?

_____ 2. What did the dove return with the second time it was sent out, Genesis 8:11?

_____ 3. The third time the dove was sent out, what happened, Genesis 8:12?

_____ 4. Why did the psalmist want wings like a dove, Psalm 55:6?

_____ 5. Who said he mourned like a dove and his eyes failed with looking upward, Isaiah 38:9-14?

_____ 6. Whom did Jeremiah tell to dwell in the rocks and be like the dove, Jeremiah 48:28?

_____ 7. Who said that the Israelites who escaped would be like doves, mourning for their iniquities, Ezekiel 7:16?

_____ 8. Whom did Hosea say was like a silly dove, Hosea 7:11?

_____ 9. At his baptism, who saw the Spirit of God descending like a dove, Matthew 3:16?

_____10. Whom did Jesus tell to go out as harmless as doves, Matthew 10:5,16?

19
Early Church Workers

Many people in the New Testament were known for something they did for or to the early church. Match the person with what he or she did.

1. Peter, Acts 2:14-41

2. Timothy, Acts 16:3

3. Rhoda, Acts 12:12-13

4. Dorcas, Acts 9:39

5. Lydia, Acts 16:13-14

6. Sapphira, Acts 5:1,8-9

7. Matthias, Acts 1:26

8. Stephen, Acts 7:59

9. Paul, Acts 13:2-3

10. Ananias, Acts 9:17-18

a. Prayed with a group of women
b. Served as a missionary
c. Was chosen to replace Judas
d. Paul's helper
e. Lied to the church
f. Preached and about three thousand came to know Jesus
g. Recognized Peter's voice and forgot to open the gate
h. Restored Paul's sight
i. Died for his faithfulness
j. Made clothes for needy people

20
Fathers

The most influential people in the family lives of the Israelites were fathers. Match each statement with the proper father.

1. Told to sacrifice his son, Genesis 22:1-2
2. Father who walked with God, Genesis 5:21
3. Blessed the wrong son, Genesis 27:22-23
4. Betrayed by his son, 2 Samuel 15:12-31
5. Lost all his children tragically, Job 1:13-15
6. Jesus raised his daughter, Mark 5:22,42
7. Father of twelve tribes, Genesis 49:28
8. Son baptized Jesus, Luke 1:13; Mark 1:9
9. Fled to Egypt with his family, Matthew 2:13
10. Son was the first king of Israel, 1 Samuel 9:3
11. First father on Earth, Genesis 4:1

a. Job
b. Joseph
c. Adam
d. Jairus
e. Isaac
f. Enoch
g. David
h. Jacob
i. Kish
j. Zechariah
k. Abraham

21
Feed Me

Almost everyone enjoys eating. Fill in the blanks with the correct food.

1. Daniel asked to be fed _____ and _____, Daniel 1:12.
2. John the Beptist fed on _____ and _____, Matthew 3:4.
3. Hiram traded Solomon cedar and fir trees in return for _____ and _____, 1 Kings 5:11.
4. The Israelites were fed _____ from heaven, Exodus 16:35.
5. Elijah was fed _____ and _____ by a raven, 1 Kings 17:6.
6. Jesus fed a multitude of people with five _____ and two _____, Mark 6:38.
7. Lazarus wanted to be fed _____ from the rich man's table, Luke 16:21.
8. The prodigal son would have fed himself the _____, Luke 15:16.
9. Joseph sold his brothers _____ during a famine so that they might be fed, Genesis 42:25.
10. Elijah assured the widow that she and her son would not run out of _____ and _____, 1 Kings 17:14.

22
Fishermen

In Bible times, people often fished for a living. Name the person in each statement.

1. The fisherman who brought a lad with five loaves and two fish to Jesus was _____, John 6:8-9.
2. A fisherman who, with his brother John, followed Jesus was _____, Matthew 4:21.
3. The fisherman who was told by Jesus to catch a fish with money in its mouth was _____, Matthew 17:26-27.
4. The man who promised to make his followers "fishers of men" was _____, Matthew 4:19.
5. The man who was blessed by God: "And the fear of you shall be . . . upon all the fishes of the seas" was _____, Genesis 9:1-2.
6. The fisherman whose two sons became disciples was _____, Matthew 4:2.
7. Two disciples who are named among those who went fishing with Peter but didn't catch anything all night were _____ and _____, John 21:2.

23
Foods

Match the food with the consumer.

1. Samson found this in a carcase, Judges 14:8
2. Gideon brought to an angel, Judges 6:19-20
3. Jesus ate after he arose, Luke 24:42
4. Esau sold birthright for, Genesis 25:34
5. The Israelites remembered, Numbers 11:5
6. Pharaoh's baker dreamed he carried in a basket, Genesis 40:17
7. David gave an Egyptian, 1 Samuel 30:11-12
8. Abraham brought to heavenly visitors, Genesis 18:8
9. Jael brought to the enemy, Judges 4:18-19
10. Fruit brought out of the land of Canaan, Numbers 13:23

a. Raisins
b. Butter
c. Honey
d. Pottage
e. Milk
f. Bakemeats
g. Broth
h. Grapes
i. Fish
j. Melons

24
Friends of Jesus

Fill in the blanks with the names of some of Jesus' friends.

1. _____, _____, and _____ were the only witnesses at both the transfiguration, Matthew 17:1-13, and the prayer at Gethsemane, Matthew 26:36-46.
2. _____ sat at Jesus' feet and listened to him, Luke 10:39.
3. Jesus raised _____ from the dead, John 11:41-44.
4. _____ expressed her belief in Jesus, John 11:24-27.
5. _____ helped bury Jesus, John 19:39-40.
6. The tomb Jesus was buried in belonged to _____, Matthew 27:57-60.
7. _____ pointed his followers to Jesus, John 3:25-36.
8. Jesus befriended _____, Luke 19:5.
9. _____ spoke to Jesus in the garden, thinking him to be the gardener, John 20:15.
10. Jesus shared a meal with friends at the home of _____, Matthew 26:6.

25
Fruits and Vegetables

Match the fruits and vegetables with the statements about them.

1. Pomegranate, 1 Kings 7:18-21
2. Lentils, Genesis 25:34
3. Wild grapes, Isaiah 5:1-2,7
4. Hyssop, Psalm 51:7
5. Fig, Luke 13:6-7
6. Cucumbers, Numbers 11:5
7. Olive oil, Exodus 30:24-25
8. Mustard seed, Luke 17:6
9. Mandrakes, Genesis 30:14-16
10. Sycomore fruit, Amos 7:14

a. Used as an antiseptic
b. Jesus used to teach that God is merciful in giving many opportunities to show our faith by our deeds
c. Jesus used to teach about faith
d. Used to make a holy ointment
e. Decorated pillars in Temple
f. Compared to the house of Israel
g. Jacob used in his stew
h. Vegetable Hebrews longed for in the wilderness
i. Amos gathered this fruit
j. Rachel bargained with Leah to have them

26
Furnishings

Houses in biblical times had few pieces of furniture. Fill in the blanks with the furniture mentioned.

1. A man on a _____ was let down through a roof to see Jesus, Luke 5:19.
2. A beggar desired to eat crumbs which fell from a rich man's _____, Luke 16:21.
3. Jehoiada made a bank from a _____ to hold the offerings, 2 Kings 12:9.
4. A great woman of Shunem and her husband prepared a room with a _____, _____, and _____ for Elisha to use, 2 Kings 4:8-10.
5. Jesus told a man sick with palsy to take up his _____ and walk, Matthew 9:6.
6. God said the Egyptians would have frogs everywhere, even in their _____, Exodus 8:3.
7. Solomon said the virtuous woman "layeth her hands to the _____," Proverbs 31:19.
8. To protect David, Michal placed an image in a _____ and said David was sick, 1 Samuel 19:13.
9. Seven men were chosen to work at _____ to free the disciples to study and preach, Acts 6:2-3.
10. No one would put a _____ under a bushel, Matthew 5:15.

27
God Called

When God calls people, they are usually at work. Match each person with what he was doing when God called him.

1. Samuel, 1 Samuel 3:10
2. David, 1 Samuel 16:11-13
3. Paul, Acts 9:2-6
4. Amos, Amos 7:14-15
5. King Saul, 1 Samuel 9:17-20
6. Matthew, Matthew 9:9
7. James and John, Matthew 4:21
8. Nehemiah, Nehemiah 1:1; 2:1
9. Peter and Andrew, Matthew 4:18
10. Elisha, 1 Kings 19:19

a. Mending nets
b. Serving the king
c. Searching for lost animals
d. Caring for sheep
e. Herdsman and gatherer of sycomore fruit
f. Journeying to persecute Christians
g. Plowing oxen
h. Collecting taxes
i. Being a priest's helper
j. Fishing

28
God Commanded

Often God's will is not easy to obey. These people experienced some of the hard-to-obey commands of God. Match the person with what God told him to do.

1. Abram (Abraham), Genesis 12:1
2. Jonah, Jonah 1:1-3
3. Hosea, Hosea 1:2
4. Moses, Exodus 14:14-16
5. Joseph, Matthew 2:13
6. Zechariah, Luke 1:13,18
7. Ananias, Acts 9:10-15
8. Peter, Acts 10:19-20
9. Noah, Genesis 6:13-14
10. Samuel, 1 Samuel 16:1-2

a. to name his unborn son "John"
b. to anoint someone else king while Saul lived
c. to enter a Gentile's home and preach
d. to cross a sea on foot
e. leave his father's house and move to a new land
f. to take a harlot for a wife
g. to preach to his enemy
h. to help a man who killed Christians
i. to build a boat on dry land
j. to take his wife and infant son to Egypt

29
Grievers

Grief is a normal emotion in life. Match the person with the cause of his grief.

1. Job, Job 30:25
2. Jesus, Isaiah 53:4
3. Mary and Martha, John 11:19
4. Mary Magdalene, John 20:15
5. Men on Emmaus road, Luke 24:17,21
6. Jonah, Jonah 4:1-3
7. David, 2 Samuel 12:16
8. Hannah, 1 Samuel 1:5-8
9. Jonathan, 1 Samuel 20:34
10. Esther, Esther 4:4-7
11. Daniel, Daniel 7:15

a. a loved one's body
b. childless state
c. visions uninterpreted
d. the poor
e. humanity
f. repentance of enemies
g. loss of a leader
h. mistreatment of a friend
i. plot to destroy the Jews
j. death of a brother
k. a sick child

30
Headlines

Read each headline below, and match it to the person most likely referred to.

1. Young Boy Slays Giant with Slingshot
2. Rejoicing Women Led by Prophetess
3. Man Survives Lions' Den
4. King Has Church Leader Killed
5. Runaway Slave Returns to Master
6. Persecutor of Christians Converted
7. Red Sea Parts for Man and Followers
8. Successor Chosen for Moses
9. Two Cities Destroyed; One Family Survives
10. Man Hung by His Own Hair
11. Woman Reports Resurrection

a. James, Acts 12:1-2

b. Moses, Exodus 14:22

c. Joshua, Joshua 1:1-6

d. Paul, Acts 9:6

e. Miriam, Genesis 15:20-21

f. Absalom, 2 Samuel 18:10

g. Daniel, Daniel 6:12-16

h. David, 1 Samuel 17:24,50

i. Mary Magdalene, John 20:18

j. Onesimus, Philemon 10-12

k. Lot, Genesis 19:16-25

31
Jesus Asked

Jesus asked many pointed questions. List the person to whom he asked each question.

_____ 1. "If I have told you earthly things, and ye believe not, how shall ye believe, if I tell you of heavenly things?" John 3:12.

_____ 2. "Whence shall we buy bread that these may eat?" John 6:5.

_____ 3. "Lovest thou me?" John 21:15.

_____ 4. "But whom say ye that I am?" Matthew 16:15.

_____ 5. "Whom seek ye?" John 18:3-5.

_____ 6. "If I have spoken evil, bear witness of the evil: but if well, why smitest thou me?" John 18:22-23.

_____ 7. "But if ye love them which love you, what reward have ye?" Matthew 5:46.

_____ 8. "What wilt thou that I should do unto thee?" Mark 10:46-51.

_____ 9. "Wherefore think ye evil in your hearts?" Matthew 9:4.

_____10. "Believe ye that I am able to do this?" Matthew 9:28.

_____11. "Wilt thou be made whole?" John 5:6-7

32
Jesus' Miracles

Match each miracle Jesus performed with the person for whom the miracle was performed.

1. A nobleman, John 4:46-53
2. A multitude of people, Matthew 15:34-36
3. Jairus, Mark 5:22-41
4. Bartimaeus, Mark 10:46-52
5. High priest's servant, Luke 22:50-51
6. Peter, Matthew 14:29
7. Widow of Nain, Luke 7:11-16
8. Mary and Martha, John 11:39-44
9. A bridegroom, John 2:1-10
10. Peter's mother-in-law, Mark 1:30-31

a. son raised from the dead
b. water became wine
c. son healed
d. brother raised from dead
e. fed with seven loaves and a few fish
f. received sight
g. fever healed
h. walked on water
i. daughter raised from dead
j. ear restored

33
Jesus' Return

One of the most speculated about events today is Jesus' return. Fill in each blank with the proper answer about the second coming of Jesus.

_____ 1. The second coming of Christ is compared to what weather condition, Matthew 24:27?

_____ 2. The second coming is compared to what night visitor, 1 Thessalonians 5:2?

_____ 3. What virtue is encouraged as we wait for the second coming, James 5:8?

_____ 4. What did Paul tell Timothy to keep until Jesus returns, 1 Timothy 6:11-12,14?

_____ 5. Whose work did Paul say would be done before Jesus' return, 2 Thessalonians 2:9?

_____ 6. Who will meet the Lord first when he returns, 1 Thessalonians 4:16?

_____ 7. What will be changed when Jesus returns, Philippians 3:21?

_____ 8. What will God do to all believers when Jesus returns, 2 Corinthians 5:10?

_____ 9. What is the last enemy to be destroyed at Jesus' return, 1 Corinthians 15:26?

_____ 10. What did Jesus say he was going to prepare for us, John 14:2?

_____ 11. In what will Jesus return, Luke 21:27?

_____ 12. What occupation did Jesus liken the judgment to, Matthew 25:32?

_____ 13. Who is the only person who knows when Jesus' return is, Matthew 24:36?

34
Jesus Taught the Disciples

Jesus spent much time instructing his disciples so that they could take over when he left the earth. Answer these questions about what Jesus taught the disciples.

1. What was the only thing Jesus told his disciples to take on mission trips, Mark 6:8? _____

2. What were the disciples to do if they were not welcome in a place, Mark 6:11? _____

3. What were the disciples to do on their mission, Luke 9:2? _____

4. What do we call the prayer Jesus taught his disciples, Matthew 6:9-13? _____

5. How did Jesus tell his disciples to treat others, Matthew 7:12? _____

6. To what two things did Jesus compare the disciples, Matthew 5:13-16? _____

7. To what did Jesus compare his relationship with his disciples, John 15:5? _____

8. What did Jesus use to teach his disciples humility, Matthew 18:1-2? _____

9. What did Jesus say he was leaving with the disciples, John 14:27? _____

10. What did Jesus tell his disciples to use as a remembrance of his body, Luke 22:19? _____

11. What did Jesus tell the disciples to do if they loved him, John 14:15? _____

35
Joseph

One of the first Bible people that children learn about is Joseph. Match the following facts about Joseph found in Genesis.

1. Home country
2. Father
3. Master
4. Oldest brother
5. New country
6. Purchasers
7. Mother
8. Grandfather
9. Temptress
10. Interpreted dreams
11. His hostage

a. Jacob, 30:25
b. Reuben, 35:23
c. Simeon, 42:24
d. Potiphar's wife, 39:7
e. Canaan, 33:18
f. Egypt, 37:36
g. Rachel, 30:22-24
h. Ishmeelites, 37:28
i. Pharaoh, 41:25
j. Laban, 29:5-7
k. Potiphar, 37:36

36
Kind Deeds

The Bible has many examples of kindness. Fill in each blank with the deed of kindness shown.

1. Abraham let Lot have first choice of _____, Genesis 13:8-12.
2. Jesus was presented _____, _____, and _____ by the Wise Men, Matthew 2:1,11.
3. The good Samaritan helped a man who was robbed by _____ up his wounds, Luke 10:30-37.
4. Jesus praised a widow because she gave _____, Luke 21:1-4.
5. Simon, a Cyrenian, carried Jesus' _____, Luke 23:26.
6. Mary anointed Jesus' feet with _____, John 12:3.
7. Boaz rewarded Ruth because of her kindness to her _____, Ruth 2:5-11.
8. David allowed Mephibosheth to _____ for Jonathan's sake, 2 Samuel 9:6-7.
9. Rahab aided the spies by letting them down _____ through a window, Joshua 2:1,15.
10. Jonathan gave David a _____, _____, _____, and _____, 1 Samuel 18:4.
11. Dorcas made _____ and _____ for widows, Acts 9:39.

37
Kings

Kings are influential in shaping the history of their nations. Match each king with the proper statement about him.

1. Built an altar, asking that a plague end
2. Carried Judah and Jerusalem into Exile
3. Built the Temple
4. Reigned three months
5. Had fifteen years added to his life
6. His hand "dried up"
7. Made a covenant before the Lord
8. Had youngest children of Bethlehem slain
9. Fell through his upper chamber
10. Gave decree to rebuild Temple
11. Threw a javelin at David

a. Jeroboam, 1 Kings 13:4
b. Ahaziah, 2 Kings 1:2
c. Solomon, 2 Chronicles 7:11
d. Darius, Ezra 6:1,8
e. David, 2 Samuel 24:25
f. Hezekiah, 2 Kings 20:5-6
g. Josiah, 2 Chronicles 34:31
h. Saul, 1 Samuel 18:10-11
i. Nebuchadnezzar, 1 Chronicles 6:15
j. Jehoiachin, 2 Kings 24:8
k. Herod, Matthew 2:16

38
Leaders

Match the leader with the activity.

1. Peter, Acts 2:1,14

2. Aaron, Exodus 32:2-4

3. Aquila and Priscilla, Acts 18:24-27

4. God, Exodus 13:21

5. Jonah, Jonah 3:4-5

6. Absalom, 2 Samuel 15:4

7. Saul, 1 Samuel 10:24

8. Paul, Acts 17:22,34

9. Joseph, Genesis 41:45-48

10. Caiaphas, John 18:14

11. Joshua, Joshua 6:2,6-7

a. Led by a cloud
b. Led the Ninevah revival
c. Preached at Pentecost
d. Led the battle of Jericho
e. Taught Apollos the things of the Lord
f. Led a conspiracy against his father
g. Led in the storing of grain for a worldwide famine
h. Led the construction of a golden calf
i. Led Jews to plot against Jesus
j. Led as first king of Israel
k. Led some Athenians to believe in Christ

39
Listeners

Match the listener and the speaker.

1. Felix, Acts 24:24
2. Eunuch, Acts 8:30-32
3. Naaman, 2 Kings 5:1-4
4. Moses, Exodus 18:17-24
5. Barak, Judges 4:6
6. Elisha, 1 Kings 19:20
7. Samson, Judges 16:16-18
8. Eve, Genesis 3:4-6
9. Ahab, 1 Kings 21:7
10. Peter, John 1:41-42
11. Zedekiah, Jeremiah 38:19-20

a. Delilah
b. Andrew
c. Jethro
d. Paul
e. Jezebel
f. Jeremiah
g. Philip
h. Elijah
i. a slave girl
j. Deborah
k. Satan

40
Loves

Match the person with the object of his or her love.

1. Christ, Ephesians 5:25
2. Father, Luke 15:20
3. God, John 3:16
4. Isaac, Genesis 27:1-4
5. Amnon, 2 Samuel 13:4
6. Young ruler, Matthew 19:22
7. Uzziah, 2 Chronicles 26:1,10
8. Jacob, Genesis 29:18
9. Scribes, Mark 13:38
10. Hosea, Hosea 3:1

a. Husbandry
b. An adulteress
c. Salutations
d. Tamar
e. World
f. Rachel
g. Savory meat
h. Prodigal son
i. Church
j. Possessions

41
Makers

Have you ever made something you were proud of? Match the following people with the things they made.

1. Ark, Genesis 6:13-14
2. House on a rock, Matthew 7:24
3. Barns, Luke 12:16-18
4. Temple, 1 Kings 6:14-17
5. Tower, Genesis 11:4-9
6. Gates, Nehemiah 3:1
7. Wells, Genesis 26:18
8. Sacrifice altar, Genesis 22:9
9. Gallows, Esther 5:14
10. Idol in a grove, 1 Kings 15:13
11. A coat, 1 Samuel 2:19

a. Maachah
b. Abraham
c. Eliashib
d. Solomon
e. Wise man
f. Noah
g. A fool
h. People of Babel
i. Isaac
j. Haman
k. Hannah

42
Medicine

God uses many methods of healing. Match the method with the person healed.

1. Jesus' fingers in ears and spit
2. Lump of figs
3. Dip in Jordan River
4. Touch by Jesus
5. Look at brass serpent
6. Spoken word of Jesus
7. Touch of Jesus' garment
8. Dip in troubled waters of pool of Bethesda
9. Prayer and laying on of hands
10. Faith of his friends

a. Centurian's servant, Matthew 8:13
b. Publius' father, Acts 28:8
c. Man with palsy, Matthew 9:2
d. Israelites' snake bites, Numbers 21:9
e. Deaf man with speech impediment, Mark 7:33
f. Peter's mother-in-law, Mark 1:30-31
g. Naaman, 2 Kings 5:14
h. Woman sick for twelve years, Mark 5:25-29
i. People around pool, John 5:4
j. Hezekiah's boils, Isaiah 38:21

43
Messianic Prophecies

The prophets wrote and spoke of the coming Messiah. Tell which prophet made the following prophecies.

1. _____ said the Messiah would be born in Bethlehem.
2. _____ said the Messiah would be born of a virgin.
3. _____ said the Messiah would be taken out of Egypt.
4. _____ said the Messiah would be a mighty prophet in word and deed.
5. _____ said the Messiah would have his hands and feet pierced.
6. _____ said the Messiah would be despised and rejected.
7. _____ said the Messiah would make a triumphal entry into Jerusalem.
8. _____ said the Messiah would be made an offering for sin.
9. _____ said soldiers would cast lots for the Messiah's garments.
10. _____ said the Messiah would be betrayed and sold for thirty pieces of silver.
11. _____ said that Jesus would suffer in silence.

44
Milestones of Jesus

Each of the following places meant something special in Jesus' life. Match the place with what happened there.

1. Bethlehem, Matthew 2:1
2. Nazareth, Matthew 2:23
3. Jerusalem, Luke 2:42
4. Jordan River, Matthew 3:13
5. Sea of Galilee, Luke 8:23-25
6. Calvary, Luke 23:33
7. Capernaum, Matthew 4:13
8. Gethsemane, Mark 14:32
9. Cana, John 2:1
10. Bethesda, John 5:2-9
11. Bethany, Luke 24:50-51

a. Attended a wedding; first miracle
b. Ascended from here
c. Center of ministry
d. Stilled a storm
e. Celebrated Passover at age twelve
f. Birthplace
g. Home
h. Baptized
i. Crucified
j. Prayed
k. Healed a man

45
Miracles

Match the miracle with the person.

1. Devils were cast out of him
2. Survived a snake bite
3. Walked on water
4. Increased the widow's oil
5. Saw a burning bush
6. Had a vision of an angel measuring Jerusalem
7. Journeyed to heaven on a whirlwind
8. Wrote about a vision of heaven
9. Turned water into wine
10. Survived a flood on a boat he built

a. Elisha, 2 Kings 4:2-6
b. John, Revelation 1:9-11
c. Noah, Genesis 8:18
d. Legion, Luke 8:30-33
e. Zechariah, Zechariah 2:1-2
f. Moses, Exodus 3:3-4
g. Paul, Acts 28:3-5
h. Peter, Matthew 14:28-29
i. Elijah, 2 Kings 1,11
j. Jesus, John 2:9

46
Mothers

Mothers have always played an important role in shaping the characters of their children. Match each mother with the proper statement.

1. Mother of all living
2. Helped son deceive his father
3. Was paid to care for her son
4. Was commended by Paul
5. Sought best for her sons
6. Wept for her children
7. Became mother to a daughter-in-law
8. Caused death of John the Baptist
9. Killed her grandsons
10. Gave her son to ministry
11. Highly favored by God

a. Rachel, Jeremiah 31:15
b. Mary, Luke 1:30
c. Eve, Genesis 3:20
d. Hannah, 1 Samuel 1:11; 2:11
e. Rebekah, Genesis 27:6-10
f. Athaliah, 2 Kings 11:1
g. Jochebed, Exodus 2:8-10; 6:20
h. Herodias, Mark 6:22-25
i. Eunice, 2 Timothy 1:5
j. Naomi, Ruth 1:16
k. Salome, Matthew 20:20; Mark 16:1

47
Murders

The people in the left column were responsible for the deaths of the people in the middle column. Match the murderer with the murdered and then, the reason for the murder.

1. Cain, Genesis 4:4-8
2. David, 2 Samuel 11:3-12
3. Joab, 2 Samuel 3:30
4. Benaiah, 1 Kings 2:29,34
5. Absalom, 2 Samuel 13:22,28-29
6. Pekah, 2 Kings 15:23-25
7. Herod, Acts 12:1-2
8. Ahimelech, 1 Samuel 22:16,18
9. Jehoiakim, Jeremiah 26:20-23
10. Jael, Judges 4:18-22

A. Amnon
B. Urijah
C. Abel
D. Uriah
E. Joab
F. James
G. Doeg
H. Pekahiah
I. Abner
J. Sisera

a. Offering
b. Revenge
c. Throne
d. Prophesy
e. Persecution
f. Solomon's instructions
g. Hatred
h. Bathsheba
i. Saul's instructions
j. Enemy

48
Natural Calamities

Regardless of where we may live, all of us are subject to natural calamities of one sort or another. Match the person with the calamity he experienced.

1. A flood
2. Drought
3. Tempest (storm)
4. Lightnings
5. Hail
6. Earthquake
7. Whirlwind
8. Black clouds and wind
9. Thunder

a. Pharaoh, Exodus 9:28
b. Elijah, 2 Kings 2:1,11
c. Samuel, 1 Samuel 7:10
d. Ahab, 1 Kings 18:45
e. Jonathan, 1 Samuel 14:13-15
f. Noah, Genesis 6:17
g. Jonah, Jonah 1:4
h. Jacob, Gen. 41:57
i. Moses, Exodus 19:16

49
Occupations

When God called the following people, they were busy working at something. Match the person with what he or she did for a living.

1. Moses, Exodus 3:1
2. Gideon, Judges 6:11
3. Elisha, 1 Kings 19:16-19
4. Lydia, Acts 16:14
5. Priscilla and Aquila, Acts 18:3
6. Zacchaeus, Luke 19
7. Luke, Colossians 4:14
8. Baruch, Jeremiah 36:4
9. Deborah, Judges 4:4
10. Esther, Esther 2:17

a. Farmer
b. Seller of purple cloth
c. Shepherd
d. Judge
e. Thresher
f. Scribe
g. Queen
h. Tentmakers
i. Tax collector
j. Doctor

50
Oil

Answer each question with the person involved with oil.

_____ 1. Who asked the wise virgins for oil for their lamps, Matthew 25:7-8?

_____ 2. Who used oil on the wounds of a man beaten by robbers, Luke 10:33-34?

_____ 3. Who multiplied the oil of a widow so she could pay her debts, 2 Kings 4:2-7?

_____ 4. What tribe received this blessing: "Let him be acceptable to his brethren, and let him dip his foot in oil," Deuteronomy 33:24?

_____ 5. To whom did Jesus say, "My head with oil thou didst not anoint: but this woman hath anointed my feet with ointment," Luke 7:43,46?

_____ 6. Who poured oil on a pillar of stone and named the place Bethel, Genesis 35:14-15?

_____ 7. Who asked a woman to pretend to be a mourner and not anoint herself with oil, 2 Samuel 14:2?

_____ 8. Who was anointed with oil by Zadok, 1 Kings 1:39?

_____ 9. To whom did Solomon give twenty thousand measures of pure oil in exchange for cedar trees, 1 Kings 5:11?

_____10. Who told a woman to make him a cake of her last meal and oil and her supply of oil and meal would not run out, 1 Kings 17:12-16?

51
Organizers

People who get things done are usually good organizers. In the Bible there are examples of people who organized. Match the person with what he organized.

1. Jethro, Exodus 18:9-24
2. The twelve, Acts 6:1-7
3. Jesus, Luke 10:1
4. Jacob, Genesis 33:1-4
5. Joshua, Joshua 6:1-7
6. David, 2 Samuel 24:1-2
7. Moses, Exodus 13:17-20
8. Gideon, Judges 7:4-7
9. Nehemiah, Nehemiah 2:17-18
10. Paul, Acts 15:40

a. suggested Moses organize judges to help him
b. organized his family when he went to meet his brother
c. organized a census of the children of Israel
d. organized seventy followers in pairs
e. organized deacons to assist them
f. organized for the defeat of Jericho
g. organized soldiers for battle by using water
h. organized a mission trip
i. organized the Israelites for a trip into the wilderness
j. organized the rebuilding of the Jerusalem wall

52
Paul's Associates

The following people were associated with Paul. Match the proper statement with the person.

1. Asked, "What must I do to be saved?" Acts 16:25-30
2. Said, "Almost thou persuadest me to be a Christian," Acts 26:28
3. Led the silversmiths in protest against Paul, Acts 19:24-25
4. Left Paul in prison in an effort to gain favor with the Jews, Acts 24:26-27
5. Sent Paul to Caesar, Acts 25:12
6. Sent with Paul to settle a dispute in Jerusalem, Acts 15:2
7. Arrested for harboring Paul, Acts 17:5
8. Guarded Paul on trip to Jerusalem for trial, Acts 27:1
9. Told Paul of a plot to kill him, Acts 23:16
10. Paul healed him of a fever, Acts 28:8
11. An orator who accused Paul before Felix, Acts 24:1-3

a. Felix
b. Julius
c. Barnabas
d. Tertullus
e. a nephew
f. jailer
g. Publius's father
h. Demetrius
i. Festus
j. Jason
k. Agrippa

53
People Jesus Helped

Everywhere Jesus went he found people with needs, and he responded in a helping way. Match the need with the appropriate scripture reference.

1. The hungry
2. The thirsty
3. The naked
4. The sick
5. The prisoner
6. The blind
7. The thief
8. The dead
9. The bereaved
10. The lost

a. John 11:43-44
b. John 3:1-3
c. Mark 1:34
d. Mark 10:51-52
e. Luke 9:13-17
f. Luke 8:27,35
g. John 11:21-27
h. Luke 23:39-43
i. John 4:10
j. Matthew 11:2-4

54
Places

Where are the following biblical places located today? Use a world atlas and Bible maps to match the biblical place in the left column with the modern location in the right column.

1. Antioch of Pisidia
2. Bethlehem
3. Rome
4. Damascus
5. Jerusalem
6. Macedonia
7. Ur
8. Thessalonica
9. Goshen
10. Ephesus

a. Asia
b. Turkey
c. Syria
d. Jordan
e. Greece
f. Yugoslavia and Greece
g. Israel and Jordan
h. Iraq
i. Italy
j. Egypt

55
Prayer Places

Wherever people are, they may call to God in prayer. Match each person with the place where he or she prayed.

1. Jesus, John 11:38-41
2. Peter and John, Acts 3:1
3. Paul and Silas, Acts 16:23-25
4. A group of women, Acts 16:13
5. Jesus, Peter, James, and John, Luke 9:28
6. Jonah, Jonah 2:1
7. Habakkuk, Habakkuk 2:1
8. David, Psalm 63:6
9. Daniel, Daniel 6:10-11
10. Hypocrites, Matthew 6:5
11. Hezekiah, 2 Kings 20:1-7

a. In a tower
b. On a mountain
c. On sick bed
d. At a grave
e. In a fish
f. In bed
g. In jail
h. At a river
i. At a window
j. In the Temple
k. On street corners

56
Prophecies Fulfilled

Using a concordance, find the prophecy that was fulfilled.

_____ 1. Paul wrote of the fulfillment of the prophecy that Jesus would be born of the "seed" of "woman," Galatians 4:4.

_____ 2. Luke wrote of the fulfillment of the prophecy that Jesus was to be from Abraham, Acts 3:25.

_____ 3. Matthew wrote of the fulfillment of the prophecy of the flight into Egypt, Matthew 2:14-15.

_____ 4. John wrote of the fulfillment of the prophecy about the rejection of Jesus, John 1:11.

_____ 5. Matthew wrote of the fulfillment of the prophecy of Jesus suffering for us, Matthew 8:17.

_____ 6. John wrote of the fulfillment of the prophecy of Jesus' bones not being broken, John 19:33.

_____ 7. The writer of Hebrews wrote of the fulfillment of the prophecy of a new covenant, Hebrews 8:8-12.

_____ 8. Paul wrote of the fulfillment of the prophecy of those God called "not my people" becoming children of God, Romans 9:26.

_____ 9. Matthew wrote of the fulfillment of the prophecy of the "stone rejected by the builders," Matthew 21:42.

_____10. Luke wrote of the fulfillment of the prophecy about kings and rulers gathering against Christ, Acts 4:25-26.

57
Praise

Many people express their joy, excitement, and sorrow by praising the Lord. Match the person with his or her statement of praise.

1. Mary, Luke 1:49

2. David, Psalm 136:1

3. Paul, 1 Corinthians 15:57

4. Daniel, Daniel 2:20

5. Jesus, Matthew 11:25

6. Nebuchadnezzar, Daniel 4:34

7. Simeon, Luke 2:25-29

8. Peter, 1 Peter 1:3

9. Jude, Jude 25

10. John, Revelation 1:6

a. "Blessed be the name of God for ever and ever: for wisdom and might are his."
b. "I blessed the most High, and I praised and honoured him that liveth for ever."
c. "Blessed be the God and Father of our Lord Jesus Christ, which according to his abundant mercy hath begotten us again unto a lively hope by the resurrection of Jesus Christ from the dead."
d. "Lord, now lettest thou thy servant depart in peace, according to thy word. For mine eyes have seen thy salvation."
e. "To the only wise God our Saviour, be glory and majesty, dominion and power, both now and ever."
f. "I thank thee, O Father . . . because thou hast hid these things from the wise and prudent, and hast revealed them unto babes."
g. "But thanks be to God, which giveth us the victory through our Lord Jesus Christ."
h. "And hath made us kings and priests unto God and his Father; to him be glory and dominion for ever and ever."
i. "For he that is mighty hath done to me great things; and holy is his name."
j. "O give thanks unto the Lord; for he is good: for his mercy endureth for ever."

58
Proverbs

Match the beginning and the ending of the Proverbs below.

1. The fear of the Lord is
2. He that hath no rule over his own spirit is
3. But the path of the just is
4. The mouth of a righteous man is
5. The law of the wise is
6. He that is slow to wrath is
7. In the fear of the Lord is
8. The highway of the upright is to
9. The name of the Lord is
10. Bread of deceit is
11. A word fitly spoken is like

a. strong confidence, 14:26.
b. a strong tower, 18:10.
c. apples of gold in pictures of silver, 25:11.
d. a fountain of life, 13:14.
e. as the shining light, that shineth more and more unto the perfect day, 4:18.
f. depart from evil, 16:17.
g. the beginning of knowledge, 1:7.
h. sweet to a man, 20:17.
i. like a city that is broken down and without walls, 25:28.
j. of great understanding, 14:29.
k. a well of life, 10:11.

59
Rebels

Each of the following people rebelled against someone. Match the rebel and the other person.

1. Cain, Genesis 4:5-9
2. Korah, Numbers 16:1-3
3. Absalom, 2 Samuel 15:14
4. Jehoiakim, 2 Kings 24:1
5. Hezekiah, 2 Kings 19:10-19
6. Saul, 1 Samuel 20:32-33
7. Esau, Genesis 27:41
8. Pharaoh, Exodus 8:19
9. Lot, Genesis 13:5-8
10. Joseph, Genesis 39:1,7-8
11. Sarai (Sarah), Genesis 16:8

a. his father, David
b. king of Assyria
c. Abram (Abraham)
d. David
e. Hagar
f. Abel
g. God
h. Potiphar's wife
i. Jacob
j. Nebuchadnezzar
k. Moses

60
Recipients

Match the person with what he received.

1. Jesus, Luke 2:25-32
2. Elisha, 2 Kings 2:13
3. Timothy, 2 Timothy 1:5
4. Solomon, 1 Chronicles 28:11 *ff.*
5. Hezekiah, 2 Kings 19:14-16
6. Bartimaeus, Mark 10:46-52
7. Judas Iscariot, Mark 14:10-11
8. Isaac, Gen. 27:9,25
9. The prodigal son, Luke 15:22
10. Joseph, Genesis 37:3
11. Solomon, 2 Chronicles 9:9

a. Received Temple plans from David
b. Received a coat from his father
c. Received sight from Jesus
d. Received silver from the priests
e. Received a letter from Shennacherib
f. Received goat meat disguised as venison from Jacob
g. Received a blessing from Simeon
h. Received spices from the queen of Sheba
i. Received a mantel from Elijah
j. Received a robe from his father
k. Received a spiritual heritage from mother and grandmother

61
Sacrifices

Sacrifices are often mentioned in the Old Testament. God commanded that sacrifices be offered on certain occasions. Match the person with the sacrifice.

1. Abel, Genesis 4:3-4
2. Noah, Genesis 8:20
3. Abraham, Genesis 22:1-19
4. Aaron, Exodus 29:38
5. Solomon, 1 Kings 12-13,62
6. David, 2 Samuel 6:12-13
7. Jesus, Hebrews 9:23-28
8. Christians, Romans 12:1
9. Jacob, Genesis 31:49-55
10. Samuel, 1 Samuel 16:2-5

a. Offer bodies as living sacrifices to God
b. offered sacrifices in the Temple
c. offered sacrifice before anointing David as king
d. offered his life as a sacrifice
e. offered the first of his flock
f. offered sacrifices daily as God instructed
g. offered sacrifice before leaving his father-in-law
h. offered sacrifice for safety of his family after the flood
i. went to offer his son for a sacrifice
j. offered sacrifice for safe return of the ark of covenant

62
Saul

Saul was the first king of Israel. Match the following facts about his life as found in 1 Samuel.

1. Anointed by
2. Played for Saul
3. Frightened by
4. Father
5. Son
6. Daughter
7. Home
8. Proclaimed king in
9. Wife
10. Place of death

a. Ahinoam, 14:50
b. David, 16:23
c. Gibeah, 10:26
d. Gilboa, 31:1,6
e. Goliath, 17:4,11
f. Gilgal, 11:15
g. Jonathan, 13:16
h. Kish, 9:3
i. Michal, 14:49
j. Samuel, 10:1

63
Says Who?

Sometimes people make statements which are long remembered by others. Fill in the blanks with the name of the person who made the statement.

_____ 1. "The Lord is my shepherd."

_____ 2. "Here am I, send me."

_____ 3. "Except a man be born again, he cannot see the kingdom of God."

_____ 4. "Believe on the Lord Jesus Christ, and thou shalt be saved."

_____ 5. "But the greatest of these is [love]."

_____ 6. "Let not your heart be troubled: ye believe in God, believe also in me."

_____ 7. "Create in me a clean heart, O God."

_____ 8. "As for me and my house, we will serve the Lord."

_____ 9. "Behold the Lamb of God, which taketh away the sin of the world."

_____10. "Silver and gold have I none, but such as I have give I thee."

64
Seafarers

Sailing was one of the main modes of transportation in Bible days. Fill in each blank with the person who sailed.

1. During a storm, _____ predicted that no life would be lost but the ship would be destroyed, Acts 27:22-26.
2. _____ took a ship to Tarshish to flee from God, Jonah 1:3.
3. Jesus found _____ and _____ with their father in a ship mending nets, Matthew 4:21.
4. Jesus was in a ship asleep when _____ awoke him because of a storm, Matthew 8:24-25.
5. _____ left a ship to walk on the water to Jesus, Matthew 14:24-29.
6. _____, _____, _____, _____, _____, and two other disciples fished all night but caught no fish, John 21:2-5.
7. _____ was instructed by God to build a ship to save him and his family from a flood, Genesis 6:13-14.
8. _____ was shipwrecked three times, 2 Corinthians 11:25.
9. _____ sent ships to Tarshish to bring back gold, silver, ivory, apes, and peacocks, 2 Chronicles 9:21.

65
Select a Person

From the answers given, select the correct person.

1. The father of John the Baptist was, Luke 1:13:
   a. Zechariah, b. Zacchaeus, c. Zephaniah.
2. Moses' sister was, Numbers 26:59:
   a. Mary, b. Miriam, c. Milcah.
3. Jesus' mother was, Luke 2:4-5:
   a. Elisabeth, b. Joanna, c. Mary.
4. The woman who was eaten by dogs was, 2 Kings 9:36-37:
   a. Jochebed, b. Jezebel, c. Joanna.
5. A woman who served as a judge was, Judges 4:4:
   a. Delilah, b. Deborah, c. Dinah.
6. A woman who lied to the church was, Acts 5:1-3,9:
   a. Sapphira, b. Salome, c. Serah.
7. A man who had a vineyard Ahab wanted was, 1 Kings 21:1:
   A. Noah, b. Naboth, c. Nicodemus.
8. A woman who left her family to live with her mother-in-law was, Ruth 1:16:
   a. Rachel, b. Rebekah, c. Ruth.
9. A young man who had a great Christian heritage was, 2 Timothy 1:5:
   a. Titus, b. Troas, c. Timothy.
10. The family of this priest was rejected by God, 1 Samuel 3:14:
    a. Elimelech, b. Eli, c. Eliphaz.

66
Seven

Seven means "complete" in biblical terms. Match each statement about seven with the proper person.

1. Had seven locks of hair
2. Labored seven years for a wife
3. Judged Israel for seven years
4. Ate grass seven times
5. Possessed seven devils
6. Dreamed of seven fat and seven lean cows
7. Built the Temple in seven years
8. Was condemned by seven princes
9. Women said her daughter-in-law was better than seven sons
10. Became king at age seven

a. Solomon, 1 Kings 6:38
b. Naomi, Ruth 4:15
c. Mary Magdalene, Mark 16:9
d. Samson, Judges 16:13
e. Pharaoh, Genesis 41:2-3
f. Ibzan, Judges 12:8-9
g. Nebuchadnezzar, Daniel 4:25,33
h. Vashti, Esther 1:14-15,19
i. Jehoash, 2 Kings 11:21
j. Jacob, Genesis 29:20

67
Sheep

One of the animals mentioned most in the Bible is sheep. Fill in the blanks with the person associated with sheep.

1. _____ was a famous shepherd boy who became a king, 1 Samuel 16:1,13.
2. _____ said that God would feed his flock like a shepherd, Isaiah 40:11.
3. _____ is the good shepherd who knows his sheep, John 10:14.
4. _____ told the shepherds about the birth of Jesus, Luke 2:8-9.
5. _____ was a shepherd while his brother was a farmer, Genesis 4:2.
6. _____ included in his daily supplies one hundred sheep, 1 Kings 4:22-23.
7. _____ led the Israelites in an offering of seven thousand sheep, 2 Chronicles 15:8-11.
8. _____ took brown sheep for his own, Genesis 30:33.
9. _____ received the first fleece of a sheep, Deuteronomy 18:4.
10. _____ gave the king of Israel many sheep as tribute, 2 Kings 3:4.

68
Sight

Sometimes we forget how very important our sight is. Fill in the blanks with the name of the person who saw something.

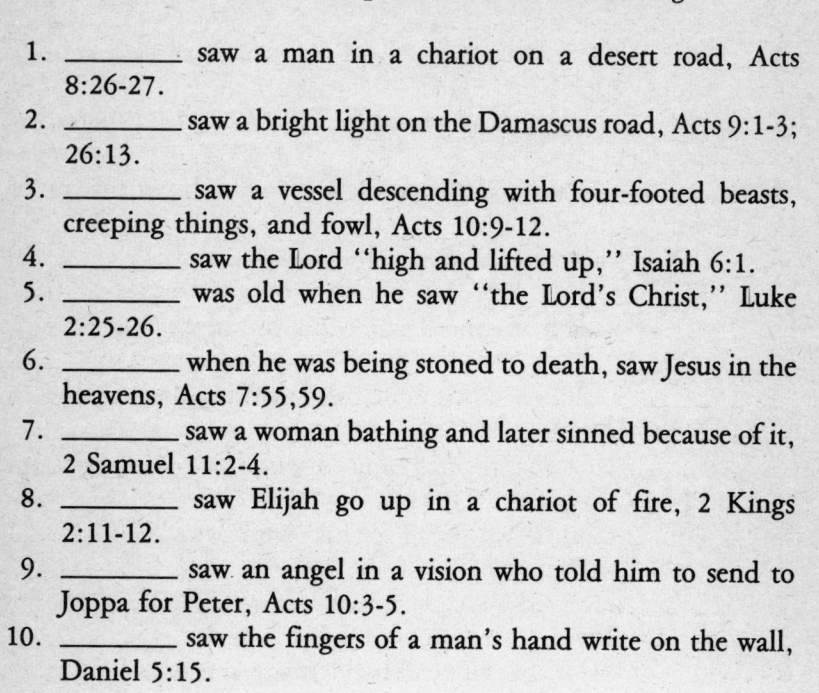

1. _____ saw a man in a chariot on a desert road, Acts 8:26-27.
2. _____ saw a bright light on the Damascus road, Acts 9:1-3; 26:13.
3. _____ saw a vessel descending with four-footed beasts, creeping things, and fowl, Acts 10:9-12.
4. _____ saw the Lord "high and lifted up," Isaiah 6:1.
5. _____ was old when he saw "the Lord's Christ," Luke 2:25-26.
6. _____ when he was being stoned to death, saw Jesus in the heavens, Acts 7:55,59.
7. _____ saw a woman bathing and later sinned because of it, 2 Samuel 11:2-4.
8. _____ saw Elijah go up in a chariot of fire, 2 Kings 2:11-12.
9. _____ saw an angel in a vision who told him to send to Joppa for Peter, Acts 10:3-5.
10. _____ saw the fingers of a man's hand write on the wall, Daniel 5:15.

69
Sins

Sometimes a person is known for one sin he or she committed. Match each person with the sin he or she committed.

1. Peter
2. Diotrephes
3. Saul
4. Saul (Paul)
5. Cain
6. Ananias
7. David
8. Noah
9. Abram (Abraham)
10. Woman and her husband (Adam and Eve)

a. Took another man's wife, 2 Samuel 12:9.
b. Lied about his wife, Genesis 12:18-19
c. Persecuted Christians, Acts 9:1
d. Ate forbidden fruit, Genesis 3:6
e. Denied Jesus, Luke 22:55-60
f. Murdered his brother, Genesis 4:8
g. Had too much pride, 3 John 9-10
h. Lied to the Holy Spirit, Acts 5:3
i. Took spoils, 1 Samuel 15:9
j. Got drunk, Genesis 9:20-21

70
Slaves

Slaves were common in Bible days. Name the person involved.

_____ 1. Who was the slave Paul wrote his friend Philemon about, Philemon 10?
_____ 2. Who was told of a way to be cured from leprosy by a slave girl, 2 Kings 5:1-3?
_____ 3. Who made slaves of the Israelites, Exodus 1:7-11?
_____ 4. Who was sold into slavery by his brothers, Genesis 37:26-28?
_____ 5. Who killed an Egyptian for hitting a Hebrew slave and then had to run to save his life, Exodus 2:11-13?
_____ 6. Who sent a slave to find his son a wife, Genesis 24:1-4?
_____ 7. Who was the slave who told David where Jonathan's son was, 2 Samuel 9:1-3?
_____ 8. Who was Elisha's slave, 2 Kings 4:12?
_____ 9. Who cut off the ear of a slave, John 18:10-11?
_____ 10. Which prophet left his slave and went a day's journey, sat under a juniper tree, and wished to die because Jezebel was trying to kill him, 1 Kings 19:1-4?
_____ 11. Who had a slave inform him that his sons and daughters had all been killed by a great wind, Job 1:18-20?

71
Soldiers

Soldiers are mentioned frequently in the Bible. Match the soldier with the correct event.

1. Centurion of an Italian cohort
2. Had eyes put out by Philistines
3. Had an army of a million men
4. Had bodyguards who could throw and shoot with either hand
5. Waged war with Ahab against Syria
6. The Syrians fled before him
7. Prayed and an angel destroyed the Assyrian army
8. Caught his head on a tree
9. Was defeated by the Chaldeans
10. Centurion assigned to guard Paul

a. Jehoshaphat, 2 Chronicles 18:1,30
b. Hezekiah, 2 Chronicles 32:20-21
c. Joab, 1 Chronicles 19:14
d. Absalom, 2 Samuel 18:9-10
e. Samson, Judges 16:20-21
f. Julius, Acts 27:1
g. Zedekiah, Jeremiah 39:5
h. Zerah, 2 Chronicles 14:9
i. Cornelius, Acts 10:1
j. David, 1 Chronicles 11:1-2

72
Statements

Match what was said with the person about whom it was said.

1. Enoch, Genesis 5:24
2. Noah, Genesis 6:8
3. King Solomon, 1 Kings 11:1
4. John the Baptist, Luke 1:17; John 1:23
5. Abraham, James 2:23
6. Demas, 2 Timothy 4:10
7. Peter, John 1:42
8. Mary, Luke 1:30
9. Job, Job 2:3
10. A rich, young man, Luke 18:23
11. Mary, Luke 10:42
12. Judas Iscariot, Matthew 26:24

a. There is none like him in the earth
b. In love with this world
c. Walked with God
d. Cephas, a stone
e. Found grace with God
f. Voice of one crying in the wilderness
g. He went away sorrowful
h. Chose the good part
i. Friend of God
j. Loved many strange women
k. Found favor with God
l. Would have been good if he had not been born

73
Sportsmen

Sports occupy much of our attention and time today. Many activities we call sports were necessary to life in Bible times. Match the person with an activity.

1. Samson
2. Paul
3. Ishmael
4. David
5. Ahimaaz
6. Benhadad
7. Jehu
8. Nimrod
9. Joab

a. Runner, 2 Samuel 18:19
b. Hunter, Genesis 10:9
c. Fighter, 1 Samuel 29:5
d. Archer, Genesis 17:20; 21:20
e. Weight lifter, Judges 16:29
f. Dart thrower, 2 Samuel 18:14
g. Swimmer, Acts 27:43-44
h. Horseman, 1 Kings 20:20
i. Racer, 2 Kings 9:20

74
They Cried Out

People often "cry out" to someone about something. Match the persons who cried out with what they cried out about.

1. The people when Jesus entered Jerusalem, John 12:13
2. The Israelites before the golden calf was made, Exodus 32:1
3. The crowd at Jesus' trial, Mark 15:13
4. The sons of the prophets to Elisha, 2 Kings 4:40
5. The disciples as Jesus walked on water, Matthew 14:26
6. The people at Jerusalem when Paul gave his testimony, Acts 22:22
7. A man with an unclean spirit, Mark 1:23-24
8. Two blind men, Matthew 20:30
9. Stephen as he was stoned, Acts 7:60
10. David upon hearing tragic news, 2 Samuel 18:33
11. Jesus on the cross, Matthew 27:46

a. "O thou man of God, there is death in the pot."
b. "My God, my God, why hast thou forsaken me?"
c. "Let us alone; what have we to do with thee, thou Jesus of Nazareth?"
d. "Up, make us gods, which shall go before us."
e. "Away with such a fellow from the earth: for it is not fit that he should live."
f. "Have mercy on us, O Lord, thou son of David."
g. "Hosanna: Blessed is the King of Israel."
h. "Lord, lay not this sin to their charge."
i. "It is a spirit."
j. "O my son Absalom, my son, my son Absalom!"
k. "Crucify him."

75
Thieves

Match the thief with the object stolen and from whom it was stolen.

1. Ahab, 1 Kings 21:14-15
2. Jacob, Genesis 25:27-34
3. Achan, Joshua 7:20-21
4. Absalom, 2 Samuel 15:6
5. Jehosheba, 2 Kings 11:2
6. Rachel, Genesis 31:19
7. Shishak, 2 Chronicles 12:9
8. Micah, Judges 17:1-2
9. Nebuchadnezzar, 2 Kings 25:1,13

A. Joash
B. images
C. birthright
D. brass pillars
E. silver
F. vineyard
G. treasures
H. hearts
I. spoils

a. Jerusalem Temple
b. the king's house
c. Mother
d. Naboth
e. Esau
f. Athaliah
g. Jericho
h. David
i. Laban

76
Titles

If we gave titles to biblical characters, the following could be supported by the facts in the Bible about them. Match titles and people.

1. The Fallen Angel
2. The Mother of All Living
3. The Wise King
4. Father of Many Nations
5. Prophet of Love
6. The Doubter
7. The Beloved Disciple
8. The Betrayer
9. The Weeping Prophet
10. The Lamb of God
11. Man Who Walked with God

a. Thomas, John 20:27
b. Enoch, Genesis 5:22
c. Jeremiah, Lamentations 1:16
d. Lucifer, Isaiah 14:12
e. Abram (Abraham) Genesis 17:4
f. John, John 13:23
g. Jesus, John 1:29
h. Eve, Genesis 3:20
i. Judas, Iscariot Matthew 10:4
j. Solomon, 1 Kings 4:29
k. Hosea, Hosea 3:1-5

77
To Whom Said?

Many times Jesus spoke to individuals rather than to the disciples or a crowd. Match what Jesus said with the person to whom it was said.

1. "Because thou has seen me, thou hast believed: blessed are they that have not seen, and yet have believed," John 20:29
2. "Lovest thou me more than these?" John 21:15.
3. "Touch me not; for I am not yet ascended to my Father: but go to my brethren, and say unto them, I ascend unto my Father," John 20:17.
4. "For the poor always ye have with you; but me ye have not always," John 12:8.
5. "I am the resurrection, and the life: he that believeth in me, though he were dead, yet shall he live," John 11:25.
6. "Go and sell that thou hast, and give to the poor, and thou shalt have treasure in heaven," Matthew 19:21.
7. "See thou tell no man; but go thy way, shew thyself to the priest, and offer . . . a testimony unto them," Matthew 8:3.
8. "Verily I say unto you, I have not found so great faith, no, not in Israel," Matthew 8:8-10.
9. "Neither do I condemn thee; go, and sin no more," John 8:11.
10. "Rise, take up thy bed, and walk," John 5:7-11.
11. "Go thy way; thy son liveth," John 4:49-50.

a. Judas Iscariot
b. Centurion
c. Rich young ruler
d. A nobleman
e. Martha
f. Thomas
g. Mary Magdalene
h. Adulterous woman
i. Simon Peter
j. Sick man
k. A leper

78
True-False Christmas Quiz

Some statements about the Christmas story are told so frequently that we assume they are correct. Answer *true* or *false* to each of the following statements. Check the references before you check your answers.

_____ 1. Mary and Joseph traveled by donkey to Bethlehem, Luke 2:3-5.

_____ 2. Jesus was laid in a manger, Luke 2:7.

_____ 3. The cattle kept Joseph and Mary company in the stable, Luke 2:7.

_____ 4. The shepherds were told to follow a star, Luke 2:11-12.

_____ 5. Angels told the shepherds of Jesus' birth, Luke 2:11.

_____ 6. Three Wise Men visited Jesus, Matthew 2:1.

_____ 7. The Wise Men found Jesus in a house, Matthew 2:11.

_____ 8. The angels sang, "Glory to God in the Highest," Luke 2:13-14.

_____ 9. The Wise Men were kings who rode on camels, Matthew 2:1-2.

_____ 10. Herod wanted to find Jesus to worship him, Matthew 2:8,12.

_____ 11. The Wise Men presented gifts of gold, frankincense, and myrrh, Matthew 2:11.

79
Trees

Trees always play an important role in history. Match these trees with the incidents below.

1. Cedar, 1 Kings 6:2,9
2. Oak, 2 Samuel 18:9
3. Fir, Psalm 104:17
4. Sycamore, Luke 19:1-4
5. Bay, Psalm 37:35
6. Mustard, Mark 4:30-32
7. Elms, Hosea 4:13
8. Juniper, 1 Kings 19:2-4
9. Fig, Matthew 24:32

a. Used to illustrate rapid growth
b. Good shade like oak and poplar
c. Jesus used to teach a lesson
d. Elijah sat under when he fled from Jezebel
e. Used in building the Temple
f. Jesus used to illustrate growth of his kingdom
g. Absalom caught his head in one
h. Storks built nests in
i. Zacchaeus climbed to see Jesus

80
Two of a Kind

Often two people will agree on something while the rest of the crowd disagree. The two people listed in the right-hand column were alike on one thing. Match the two with how they were alike.

1. Walked on water
2. Dogs licked their blood
3. Slew a lion
4. Fell from a window
5. Appeared at transfiguration
6. Were first two disciples
7. Were Lazarus' kin
8. Became friends at Jesus' trial
9. Were let down over a wall
10. Gave good reports of the Promised Land

a. David and Paul, 1 Samuel 19:12; Acts 9:25
b. Mary and Martha, John 11:19
c. Jesus and Peter, Matthew 14:29
d. Joshua and Caleb, Numbers 14:6-8
e. Ahaziah and Eutychus, 2 Kings 1:2; Acts 20:9
f. Benaiah and Samson, 2 Samuel 23:20; Judges 14:5-6
g. Ahab and Jezebel, 1 Kings 22:37-38; 2 Kings 9:33-36
h. Moses and Elias (Elijah), Matthew 17:2-3
i. Peter and Andrew, Matthew 4:18-20
j. Herod and Pilate, Luke 23:12

81
Unique Items

Sometimes a possession makes a person stand out. Match the unique item with the person who owned it.

1. A hole in the ear, Exodus 21:6
2. A crippled limb, Genesis 32:24-25
3. A thorn in the flesh, 2 Corinthians 12:7
4. Empty lamps, Matthew 25:3
5. A colorful coat, Genesis 37:3
6. A seamless robe, John 19:23-24
7. Long-lasting shoes, Deuteronomy 29:5
8. Sightless eyes, Judges 16:21-22
9. Seven hundred wives, 1 Kings 11:3
10. Five husbands, but not one, John 4:18
11. A harlot wife, Hosea 1:2
12. A withered hand, 1 Kings 13:4

a. Paul
b. Jesus
c. A lifetime slave
d. Solomon
e. Jeroboam
f. Hebrews
g. Joseph
h. Jacob
i. Hosea
j. Samson
k. Foolish virgins
l. Samaritan woman

82
Unusual Experiences

Some people experience the unusual. Match the person with his experience.

1. Moses
2. Paul
3. Jacob
4. Stephen
5. Joshua
6. Balaam
7. Elisha
8. Hebrews
9. Naaman
10. Hezekiah
11. Gideon

a. Stoning mob, Acts 7:59
b. Parting sea, Exodus 14:21
c. Wet and dry fleece, Judges 6:36-40
d. Talking donkey, Numbers 2:27-28
e. Burning bush, Exodus 3:2
f. Reversing sundial, 2 Kings 20:10-11
g. Dipping in muddy water, 2 Kings 5:11-14
h. Blinding light, Acts 9:3
i. Fighting angel, Genesis 32:24
j. Sun standing still, Joshua 10:12-13
k. Swimming axe head, 2 Kings 6:1-6

83
Uses of Oil

There were many uses for oil in the Bible. Match the use and user.

1. Wise virgins
2. Jacob
3. Solomon
4. Elijah
5. Samaritan man
6. Samuel
7. Huram
8. A widow
9. Moses
10. Israelites
11. Issachar

a. Anointing a king, 1 Samuel 16:1
b. Bathing, 2 Chronicles 2:10-11
c. Celebrating joy, 1 Chronicles 12:39-40
d. Consecrating a place, Genesis 35:14
e. Cooking, 1 Kings 17:12-16
f. Doctoring, Luke 10:34
g. Blessing a tribe, Deuteronomy 33:24
h. Exchanging for cedar, 1 Kings 5:10-11
i. Lighting lamps, Matthew 25:7-8
j. Paying debts, 2 Kings 4:2-7
k. Offering, Numbers 15:10

84
Valentines

If you were asked to pick out people who might have sent valentines during biblical days, who would you pick? Match the person with his or her likely valentine.

1. Jacob, Genesis 29:18
2. Ruth, Ruth 4:13
3. Zipporah, Exodus 2:21
4. Bathsheba, 2 Samuel 12:24
5. Rebekah, Genesis 24:67
6. Samson, Judges 16:4
7. Elkanah, 1 Samuel 1:8
8. Abraham, Genesis 17:15
9. Elimelech, Ruth 1:2
10. Joseph, Matthew 1:24-25

a. Isaac
b. Sarah
c. Rachel
d. Mary
e. Boaz
f. Delilah
g. Naomi
h. Hannah
i. Moses
j. David

85
Wash

One of the necessary activities of human beings is washing. Match the person with the kind of washing he or she did.

1. Mary, John 12:3
2. Pilate, Matthew 27:24
3. A blind man, John 9:7
4. Job, Job 9:30-31
5. David, Psalm 51:7
6. Jeremiah, Jeremiah 4:14
7. Jesus, John 13:5
8. Peter, John 13:9
9. Pharaoh's daughter, Exodus 2:5-6
10. Elders, Deuteronomy 21:6-7

a. wanted Jesus to wash his whole body
b. told the Israelites they could be saved by washing their hearts from wickedness
c. washed Jesus' feet with ointment
d. found a baby when she came to wash in a river
e. washed in the pool of Siloam
f. prayed, "Wash me, and I shall be whiter than snow."
g. washed the disciples' feet
h. said washing in snow water could not make him clean
i. washed his hands to rid himself of guilt
j. washed their hands to show innocence

86
Water

Without water no living thing can exist. Answer each statement with the name of the person involved with water.

1. _____ and _____ turned water to blood, Exodus 7:20.
2. _____ baptized with water, Matthew 3:11.
3. _____ moved upon the face of the waters, Genesis 1:2.
4. _____ said to "let judgment run down as waters," Amos 5:24.
5. _____ commanded his chariot to stop so he could be baptized in water, Acts 8:36.
6. _____ said one had to be born of water and the Spirit to enter the kingdom of God, John 3:5.
7. _____ drew water from a rock, Exodus 17:5-6.
8. _____ lay beside a pool waiting for the moving of the water, John 5:7.
9. _____ had water poured over his sacrifice until it filled the trench around the altar, 1 Kings 18:30,35.
10. _____ lived on a boat many months because of a flood, Genesis 7:1,24.

87
Wells

Wells were a major source of water in biblical times. Match the person with the proper statement about wells.

1. Herdsmen of Gerar, Genesis 26:20
2. Isaac, Genesis 26:18
3. Jesus, John 4:6-14
4. Uzziah, 2 Chronicles 26:9-10
5. Isaiah, Isaiah 12:3
6. Abraham's servant, Genesis 24:10-13
7. Joseph, Genesis 49:22
8. Moses, Numbers 21:16
9. David, 2 Samuel 23:15-17
10. Marah, Exodus 15:23

a. Produced bitter water
b. Was given water at the well in Beer
c. Fought over a well
d. Witnessed to a woman at a well
e. Built towers and wells in the desert
f. Waited at a well to find Isaac a wife
g. Refused to drink water because three men risked their lives getting it for him
h. Was blest as "a fruitful bough by a well"
i. Prophesied that people would "draw water out of the wells of salvation"
j. Dug again the wells of his father

88
What Shall I Do?

Often in desperation, people cry, What shall I do? Match the person with the question.

1. Jailer, Acts 16:30
2. Rich young ruler, Matthew 19:16
3. Pilate, Matthew 27:22
4. Rich man, Luke 12:17
5. Lord of the vineyard, Luke 20:13
6. Paul, Acts 9:6
7. Isaac, Genesis 27:37
8. Moses, Exodus 17:4
9. Job, Job 31:14
10. Rebekah, Genesis 27:46

a. "What shall I do then with Jesus?"
b. "What shall I do? I will send my beloved son: it may be they will reverence him."
c. "What shall I do now unto thee my son?"
d. "What then shall I do when God riseth up? . . . what shall I answer him?"
e. "If Jacob take a wife of . . . the daughters of the land, what good shall my life do me?"
f. "What shall I do unto this people?"
g. "Lord, what wilt thou have me to do?"
h. "What shall I do, because I have no room where to bestow my fruits?"
i. "Good Master, what good thing shall I do, that I may have eternal life?"
j. "Sirs, what must I do to be saved?"

89
What's In a Name?

Biblical names usually have a significance. Match each name with its meaning.

1. Ishmael, Genesis 16:11
2. Eve, Genesis 3:20
3. Jesus, Matthew 1:21
4. Cain, Genesis 4:1
5. Noah, Genesis 5:29
6. Sarah, Genesis 17:16
7. Mara, Ruth 1:20
8. Reuben, Genesis 29:32
9. Loammi, Hosea 1:9
10. Emmanuel, Matthew 1:23

a. "The Almighty hath dealt very bitterly with me"
b. "I have gotten a man from the Lord"
c. "God with us"
d. "This same shall comfort us concerning our work and toil"
e. "Because the Lord hath heard thy affliction"
f. "Surely the Lord hath looked upon my affliction"
g. "For he shall save his people from their sins"
h. "She shall be a mother of nations"
i. "Because she was the mother of all living"
j. "For ye are not my people, and I will not be your God"

90
Wheels

Wheels are important to society. Identify the people involved in each of these questions.

_____ 1. Whose chariots lost their wheels because God would not let them follow his people?

_____ 2. Who was the mother who asked why her son's chariot wheels tarried?

_____ 3. Who saw a wheel in a wheel in the sky?

_____ 4. Who had a dream about burning wheels?

_____ 5. Who did the psalmist want God to make like a wheel?

_____ 6. Who used the potter and his wheel to illustrate how God wants to mold his people?

_____ 7. Who built a house with ten bases of brass and each base had four brasen wheels?

_____ 8. Who had a vision of a man removing fire from a wheel?

_____ 9. Who did Ezekiel say God would send to punish Tyrus and cause the walls to shake at the noise of wheels?

_____ 10. Who did Nahum say God would punish because of their wickedness by letting "the noise of the rattling of the wheels" bring destruction?

91
Where in the Bible?

It is important to know where certain passages are located in the Bible. See how many of these passages you can locate.

_____ 1. In what books of the Bible are the Ten Commandments found?

_____ 2. In what book of the Bible are 150 songs to be sung with stringed instruments?

_____ 3. In what book of the Bible do we find many wise sayings of Solomon?

_____ 4. In what book of the Bible do we find the story of how God sent Jonah to preach in Nineveh?

_____ 5. In what book of the Bible do we find the history of the first churches after Jesus' ascension?

_____ 6. In what book of the Bible do we find the battle of Jericho?

_____ 7. In what book of the Bible do we find the story of a queen who saved her people?

_____ 8. In what book of the Bible do we find the story of a man in a lion's den?

_____ 9. In what book of the Bible do we find Jesus' Sermon on the Mount?

_____ 10. In what book of the Bible do we find the creation story?

_____ 11. In what book of the Bible do we find the story of a runaway slave who returned to his master?

92
Where Jesus Prayed

Jesus prayed before each major task he faced. List the places or circumstances when Jesus prayed.

1. On a _____, Jesus prayed all night before he chose the twelve disciples, Luke 6:12-13.
2. At _____, Jesus prayed that God would remove the "cup" from him if it were possible, Mark 14:32-36.
3. In a _____, Jesus prayed before he fed five thousand people, Matthew 14:13-21.
4. Jesus prayed at a _____, John 11:40-44.
5. When he was _____, Jesus prayed, Luke 3:21.
6. At _____, Jesus prayed for forgiveness for those who crucified him, Luke 23:33-34.
7. When he was _____, Jesus prayed the Model Prayer Matthew 5:1; 6:9.
8. In a _____, Jesus thanked God for the food, and two traveling companions suddenly recognized him, Luke 24:28-31.
9. In the _____, Jesus took bread and blessed it, thereby instituting the Lord's Supper, Luke 22:16-20.
10. On the coasts of _____, children were brought to Jesus for him to pray for them, Matthew 19:1-14.

93
Who Did It?

Human beings are busy creatures. Match each person with what he did.

1. Named all the animals, Genesis 2:20
2. Built an ark, Genesis 6:13-14,22
3. Prepared a meal for Jesus, Luke 10:40
4. Introduced Paul to the Jerusalem church, Acts 9:27
5. Was in business with her husband, Acts 18:2-3
6. Stilled a storm, Mark 4:39
7. Walked on water, Matthew 14:29
8. Received a beautiful coat, Genesis 37:3
9. Killed a giant, 1 Samuel 17:42-43
10. Found a baby in a basket, Exodus 2:5
11. Burned Jeremiah's scroll, Jeremiah 36:20

a. Barnabas
b. Jesus
c. David
d. Adam
e. Jehoiakim
f. Joseph
g. Pharaoh's daughter
h. Noah
i. Peter
j. Priscilla
k. Martha

94
Who Said It?

We are often known by something that we say. Fill in the blanks with the person who made the statement.

_____ 1. "I indeed baptize you with water unto repentance: but he that cometh after me is mightier than I, whose shoes I am not worthy to bear," Matthew 3:11.

_____ 2. "How is it that ye sought me? wist ye not that I must be about my Father's business?" Luke 2:49.

_____ 3. "Choose you this day whom ye will serve . . . but as for me and my house, we will serve the Lord," Joshua 24:15.

_____ 4. "For I know that my redeemer liveth, and that he shall stand at the latter day upon the earth," Job 19:25.

_____ 5. "Give me now wisdom and knowledge, that I may go out and come in before this people," 2 Chronicles 1:10.

_____ 6. "Thou art the Christ, the Son of the living God," Matthew 16:16.

_____ 7. "And if I perish, I perish," Esther 4:16.

_____ 8. "Behold, to obey is better than sacrifice, and to harken than the fat of rams," 2 Samuel 15:22.

_____ 9. "Come, see a man, which told me all things that ever I did: is not this the Christ?" John 4:29.

_____10. "I believe that thou art the Christ, the Son of God, which should come into the world," John 11:27.

95
Widows

Widows in the Bible often had great difficulty managing. Answer each question about a widow.

_____ 1. Which widow took off her widow's garment, veiled her face, and her father-in-law thought she was a harlot, Genesis 38:13-15?

_____ 2. Which widow had two widowed daughters-in-law, Ruth 1:3-5?

_____ 3. Which widow had a son who witnessed the prediction of the division of Solomon's kingdom, 1 Kings 11:26-31?

_____ 4. Which widow praised God when she saw the infant Jesus, Luke 2:36-38?

_____ 5. Why did Jesus say a widow had given more than anyone else, Mark 12:42-44?

_____ 6. Which widow made a living for herself and her widowed mother-in-law, Ruth 2:2?

_____ 7. What did Jesus do for a weeping widow in a funeral procession, Luke 7:12-15?

_____ 8. Who pretended to be a widow and spoke to the king in behalf of Joab, 2 Samuel 14:2,5?

_____ 9. What happened when some people in the early church complained that widows were being neglected, Acts 6:1-3?

_____10. Which widow left her mother-in-law and went back to her family, Ruth 1:4?

96
Witnesses

A witness is one who testifies to what he knows. Answer each question by telling who the witness was.

_____ 1. Who witnessed to a man in a chariot, Acts 8:31?

_____ 2. Who sang in jail and witnessed to a jailer, Acts 16:29-31?

_____ 3. Who was stoned to death as a result of his witnessing, Acts 7:56-60?

_____ 4. Who witnessed to a king named Agrippa, Acts 26:1-7?

_____ 5. Who witnessed in a lion's den, Daniel 6:22?

_____ 6. Who witnessed of God's love by sewing for needy people, Acts 9:36?

_____ 7. Who witnessed to his brother saying, "We have found . . . the Christ," John 1:40-41?

_____ 8. Who witnessed in the wilderness, crying, "Repent," Matthew 3:1-2?

_____ 9. Who were the two men who had witnessed Jesus' resurrection, one of whom took the place of Judas Iscariot, Acts 1:22-23?

_____ 10. Who described himself as "a witness of the sufferings of Christ," 1 Peter 5:1?

_____ 11. Who witnessed to his friend saying, "We have found him, of whom Moses in the law, and the prophets, did write," John 1:45?

_____ 12. Who were two men who were called gods and used the occasion to witness of the living God, Acts 14:12-15?

_____ 13. Who witnessed to Apollos showing "him the ways of God more perfectly," Acts 18:24-26?

97
Women

Fill in the blanks with the correct name of the woman.

1. After _____ husband died, she became David's wife, 1 Samuel 25:39-42.
2. Abraham told people _____ was his sister, Genesis 12:11-13.
3. Jacob had twelve sons and a daughter named _____, Genesis 34:1.
4. Among other believers, Paul saluted _____ in his letter to the Roman Christians, Romans 16:15.
5. The _____ visited Solomon, 1 Kings 10:1-2.
6. _____ spoke the word of God to Hilkiah the priest, 2 Kings 22:14-15.
7. _____ instructed her daughter to ask for John the Baptist's head, Matthew 14:6-8.
8. Jesus said to _____: "Woman, behold thy son," John 19:26.
9. Mary's cousin, _____, conceived a son in her old age, Luke 1:36.
10. _____ faith kept her from perishing with unbelievers, Hebrews 11:31.
11. _____ saved her people from extinction, Esther 8:7.

98
Women in the Headlines

The women listed below might have made the headlines in the local paper of Bible times (if there had been one). Match the headline with the woman.

1. Woman Kills Man with Nail
2. Woman Healed by Prayer
3. Virgin Has a Son
4. Woman Predicts Man's Death
5. Woman Returns to Bethlehem with daughter-in-law
6. Woman Gleans Corn in Relative's field
7. Mother Helps Son Deceive Father
8. Son Given to Temple Service by Mother
9. Woman Slays Prophets
10. Woman Among First to Acclaim Christ

a. Anna, Luke 2:36-38
b. Rebekah, Genesis 27:6-30
c. Ruth, Ruth 2:2-3
d. Jael, Judges 4:21
e. Mary, Luke 1:26-31; 2:4-7
f. Miriam, Numbers 12:10-15
g. Hannah, 1 Samuel 1:20-28
h. Jezebel, 1 Kings 18:4,13
i. Naomi, Ruth 1:19
j. Deborah, Judges 4:49

99
Wood

The kind of wood used in building is very important. Different woods have qualities which make them more suitable to certain construction. Name the wood used in building in each case.

1. The ark of the covenant was built of _____ wood, Deuteronomy 10:1-3.
2. King David's house was built of _____ wood, 2 Samuel 7:2.
3. Solomon's Temple was built of _____ wood, 1 Kings 6:15.
4. The cherubim, posts, and doors of the Temple were built of _____, 1 Kings 6:23,31-33.
5. The floors of the Temple were made from _____ wood, 1 Kings 6:15.
6. Ships were made from _____ wood with masts of _____, Ezekiel 27:5.
7. Ship oars were made from _____; Ezekiel 27:6.
8. Musical instruments were made from _____ wood, 2 Samuel 6:5.
9. Booths for the Feast of Tabernacles were made from _____, _____, _____, and _____ wood, Nehemiah 8:15.
10. The altar in the tabernacle was made of _____ wood, Exodus 27:1.
11. Noah's ark was built with _____ wood, Genesis 6:14.
12. Solomon's house was built of _____ wood, 1 Kings 7:1-3.

100 Years

One way to measure time is in years. Answer the questions with the number of years.

_____ 1. How many years did it take Solomon to build the Temple, 1 Kings 6:38?

_____ 2. How many years old was Jesus when he attended the Passover feast, Luke 2:42?

_____ 3. How many years did the Israelites wander in the wilderness, Numbers 14:33?

_____ 4. How many years did Methuselah live, Genesis 5:27?

_____ 5. How many years did Abraham live before Isaac was born, Genesis 21:5?

_____ 6. How many years did the woman whom Jesus healed have a crooked back, Luke 13:11?

_____ 7. How many years had Sarah lived when Isaac was born, Genesis 17:17?

_____ 8. How many years had the woman with "an issue of blood" been sick, Matthew 9:20?

_____ 9. How many years had Mahlon and Chilion lived in Moab, Ruth 1:1,4-5?

_____ 10. How many years did Eli judge Israel, 1 Samuel 4:16-18?

_____ 11. How many years did it not rain on the Israelites when Elijah asked God to withold the rain, Luke 4:25?

_____ 12. How many years was Paul a house prisoner, Acts 28:30?

_____ 13. How many years had Noah lived when Shem, Ham, and Japheth were born, Genesis 5:32?

Answers

1. 1-d; 2-g; 3-e; 4-i; 5-h; 6-a; 7-k; 8-j; 9-f; 10-c; 11-b
2. 1-h; 2-j; 3-i; 4-f; 5-d; 6-a; 7-e; 8-c; 9-g; 10-b
3. 1-e; 2-b; 3-a; 4-d; 5-f; 6-c; 7-h; 8-i; 9-g;
4. 1-d; 2-g; 3-i; 4-h; 5-a; 6-e; 7-k; 8-c; 9-j; 10-f; 11-b
5. 1-b; 2-c; 3-a; 4-e; 5-d; 6-f; 7-i; 8-j; 9-h; 10-g
6. 1-c; 2-e; 3-d; 4-b; 5-a; 6-f; 7-j; 8-g; 9-h; 10-i
7. 1-h; 2-j; 3-k; 4-i; 5-c; 6-g; 7-d; 8-f; 9-a; 10-e; 11-b
8. 1. Ishmael; 2. Saul; 3. Jonathan; 4. The king of Israel (Ahab); 5. Josiah; 6. Job; 7. Elisha; 8. Isaiah; 9. David; 10. Isaac; 11. Joshua
9. 1. Esaias (Isaiah); 2. Israelites; 3. Elijah; 4. Joshua; 5. Joseph; 6. Philistines; 7. Sisera; 8. Zimri; 9. Sennacherib; 10. Naaman; 11. David
10. 1-e; 2-j; 3-f; 4-i; 5-g; 6-h; 7-a; 8-b; 9-d; 10-c
11. 1. Peter; 2. Ananias; 3. Philip; 4. The apostles; 5. Stephen; 6. Esaias (Isaiah); 7. Barnabas; 8. The Spirit of the Lord; 9. Saul; 10. Simon
12. 1. Nazareth; 2. Gabriel; 3. Bethlehem; 4. Manger; 5. The babe; 6. Mary; 7. A star; 8. A house; 9. God; 10. An angel
13. 1. swine; 2. ant; 3. ostrich; 4. sparrows; 5. hen; 6. eagles; 7. cattle; 8. horse; 9. sheep; 10. lion
14. 1-f; 2-k; 3-e; 4-i; 5-g; 6-h; 7-j; 8-b; 9-c; 10-d; 11-a
15. 1. Moses, Numbers 11:15; 2. Jonah, Jonah 4:3; 3. Elijah, 1 Kings 19:4; 4. Isaiah, Isaiah 6:5; 5. Saul, 1 Samuel 28:15; 6. Mordecai, Esther 4:1; 7. Mary Magdalene, John 20:13
16. 1-e; 2-d; 3-g; 4-j; 5-i; 6-k; 7-b; 8-f; 9-c; 10-h; 11-a
17. 1. Philip and Nathaniel; 2. Matthew; 3. Peter, Andrew, James, and John; 4. Judas Iscariot; 5. James; 6. Thaddaeus; 7. Thomas; 8. the Canaanite; 9. Matthias
18. 1. Noah; 2. an olive branch; 3. It did not return; 4. to fly away to rest; 5. Hezekiah; 6. inhabitants of Moab; 7. Ezekiel; 8. Ephraim; 9. Jesus; 10. the twelve
19. 1-f; 2-d; 3-g; 4-j; 5-a; 6-e; 7-c; 8-i; 9-b; 10-h
20. 1-k; 2-f; 3-e; 4-g; 5-a; 6-d; 7-h; 8-j; 9-b; 10-i; 11-c
21. 1. pulse (vegetables) and water; 2. locust and wild honey; 3. wheat and oil; 4. manna; 5. bread and flesh; 6. loaves and fish; 7. crumbs; 8. swine's food; 9. corn (wheat); 10. meal and oil
22. 1. Andrew; 2. James; 3. Peter; 4. Jesus; 5. Noah; 6. Zebedee; 7. Thomas and Nathaniel
23. 1-c; 2-g; 3-i; 4-d; 5-j; 6-f; 7-a; 8-b; 9-e; 10-h
24. 1. Peter, James, and John; 2. Mary; 3. Lazarus; 4. Martha; 5. Nicodemus; 6. Joseph of Arimathea; 7. John the Baptist; 8. Zacchaeus; 9. Mary Magdalene; 10. Simon the leper
25. 1-e; 2-g; 3-f; 4-a; 5-b; 6-h; 7-d; 8-c; 9-j; 10-i
26. 1. couch; 2. table; 3. chest; 4. table, bed, and stool; 5. bed; 6. ovens; 7. spindle; 8. bed; 9. tables; 10. candle (lamp)
27. 1-i; 2-d; 3-f; 4-e; 5-c; 6-h; 7-a; 8-b; 9-j; 10-g
28. 1-e; 2-g; 3-f; 4-d; 5-j; 6-a; 7-h; 8-c; 9-i; 10-b;
29. 1-d; 2-e; 3-j; 4-a; 5-g; 6-f; 7-k; 8-b; 9-h; 10-i; 11-c
30. 1-h; 2-e; 3-g; 4-a; 5-j; 6-d; 7-b; 8-c; 9-k; 10-f; 11-i

31 1. Nicodemus; 2. Philip; 3. Peter; 4. disciples; 5. Judas Iscariot; 6. officer at trial; 7. people at Sermon on Mount; 8. Bartimaeus; 9. scribes; 10. two blind men; 11. sick man at a pool
32 1-c; 2-e; 3-i; 4-f; 5-j; 6-h; 7-a; 8-d; 9-b; 10-g
33 1. lightning; 2. thief; 3. patience; 4. commandment; 5. Satan's; 6. the dead in Christ; 7. our bodies; 8. judge them; 9. death; 10. a place; 11. a cloud; 12. a shepherd; 13. the Father
34 1. a walking stick (staff); 2. shake the dust off of their feet; 3. preach the kingdom of God and heal the sick; 4. the Lord's Prayer; 5. "Whatsoever ye would that men should do to you, do ye even so to them"; 6. salt and light; 7. vine and branches; 8. a little child; 9. his peace; 10. bread; 11. keep his commandments
35 1-e; 2-a; 3-k; 4-b; 5-f; 6-h; 7-g; 8-j; 9-d; 10-i; 11-c
36 1. land; 2. gold, frankincense, and myrrh; 3. binding; 4. all she had; 5. cross; 6. ointment; 7. mother-in-law; 8. eat at his table; 9. by a cord; 10. robe, sword, bow, and girdle; 11. coats, garments
37 1-e; 2-i; 3-c; 4-j; 5-f; 6-a; 7-g; 8-k; 9-b; 10-d; 11-h
38 1-c; 2-h; 3-e; 4-a; 5-b; 6-f; 7-j; 8-k; 9-g; 10-i; 11-d
39 1-d; 2-g; 3-i; 4-c; 5-j; 6-h; 7-a; 8-k; 9-e; 10-b; 11-f
40 1-i; 2-h; 3-e; 4-g; 5-d; 6-j; 7-a; 8-f; 9-c; 10-b
41 1-f; 2-e; 3-g; 4-d; 5-h; 6-c; 7-i; 8-b; 9-j; 10-a; 11-k
42 1-e; 2-j; 3-g; 4-f; 5-d; 6-a; 7-h; 8-i; 9-b; 10-c
43 1. Micah, Micah 5:2; 2. Isaiah, Isaiah 7:14; 3. Hosea, Hosea 11:1; 4. Moses, Deuteronomy 18:18-19; 5. David, Psalm 22:16, 6. Isaiah, Isaiah 53:3; 7. Zechariah, Zechariah 9:9; 8. Isaiah, Isaiah 53:10; 9. David, Psalm 22:18; 10. Zechariah, Zechariah 11:12-13; 11. Isaiah, Isaiah 53:7
44 1-f; 2-g; 3-e; 4-h; 5-d; 6-i; 7-c; 8-j; 9-a; 10-k; 11-b
45 1-d; 2-g; 3-h; 4-a; 5-f; 6-e; 7-i; 8-b; 9-j; 10-c
46 1-c; 2-e; 3-g; 4-i; 5-k; 6-a; 7-j; 8-h; 9-f; 10-d; 11-b
47 1-C-a; 2-D-h; 3-I-b; 4-E-f; 5-A-g; 6-H-c; 7-F-e; 8-G-i; 9-B-d; 10-J-j
48 1-f; 2-h; 3-g; 4-i; 5-a; 6-e; 7-b; 8-d; 9-c
49 1-c; 2-e; 3-a; 4-b; 5-h; 6-i; 7-j; 8-f; 9-d; 10-g
50 1. the foolish virgins; 2. a Samaritan man; 3. Elisha; 4. Asher; 5. Simon; 6. Jacob; 7. Joab; 8. Solomon; 9. Hiram; 10. Elijah
51 1-a; 2-e; 3-d; 4-b; 5-f; 6-c; 7-i; 8-g; 9-j; 10-h
52 1-f; 2-k; 3-h; 4-a; 5-i; 6-c; 7-j; 8-b; 9-e; 10-g; 11-d
53 1-e; 2-i; 3-f; 4-c; 5-j; 6-d; 7-h; 8-a; 9-g; 10-b
54 1-b; 2-d; 3-i; 4-c; 5-g; 6-f; 7-h; 8-e; 9-j; 10-a
55 1-d; 2-j; 3-g; 4-h; 5-b; 6-e; 7-a; 8-f; 9-i; 10-k; 11-c
56 1. Genesis 3:15; 2. Genesis 22:18; 3. Hosea 11:1; 4. Isaiah 53:5; 5. Isaiah 53:4-5; 6. Psalm 34:20; 7. Jeremiah 31:31-34; 8. Hosea 1:10; 9. Psalm 118:22-23; 10. Psalm 2:1-2
57 1-i; 2-j; 3-g; 4-a; 5-f; 6-b; 7-d; 8-c; 9-e; 10-h
58 1-g; 2-i; 3-e; 4-k; 5-d; 6-j; 7-a; 8-f; 9-b; 10-h; 11-c
59 1-f; 2-k; 3-a; 4-j; 5-b; 6-d; 7-i; 8-g; 9-c; 10-h; 11-e
60 1-g; 2-i; 3-k; 4-a; 5-e; 6-c; 7-d; 8-f; 9-j; 10-b; 11-h
61 1-e; 2-h; 3-i; 4-f; 5-b; 6-j; 7-d; 8-a; 9-g; 10-c
62 1-j; 2-b; 3-e; 4-h; 5-g; 6-i; 7-c; 8-f; 9-a; 10-d

63 1. David, Psalm 23:1; 2. Isaiah, Isaiah 6:8; 3. Jesus, John 3:3; 4. Paul and Silas, Acts 16:31; 5. Paul, 1 Corinthians 13:13; 6. Jesus, John 14:1; 7. David, Psalm 51:10; 8. Joshua, Joshua 24:1,15; 9. John the Baptist, John 1:29; 10. Peter, Acts 3:6

64 1. Paul; 2. Jonah; 3. James and John; 4. the disciples; 5. Peter; 6. Peter, Thomas, Nathaniel, James, and John; 7. Noah; 8. Paul; 9. Solomon

65 1-a; 2-b; 3-c; 4-b; 5-b; 6-a; 7-b; 8-c; 9-c; 10-b

66 1-d; 2-j; 3-f; 4-g; 5-c; 6-e; 7-a; 8-h; 9-b; 10-i

67 1. David; 2. Isaiah; 3. Jesus; 4. An angel; 5. Abel; 6. Solomon; 7. Asa; 8. Jacob; 9. Priests; 10. Mesha

68 1. Philip; 2. Saul; 3. Peter; 4. Isaiah; 5. Simeon; 6. Stephen; 7. David; 8. Elisha; 9. Cornelius; 10. Belshazzar

69 1-e; 2-g; 3-i; 4-c; 5-f; 6-h; 7-a; 8-j; 9-b; 10-d

70 1. Onesimus; 2. Naaman; 3. Pharaoh; 4. Joseph; 5. Moses; 6. Abraham; 7. Ziba; 8. Gehazi; 9. Peter; 10. Elijah; 11. Job

71 1-i; 2-e; 3-h; 4-j; 5-a; 6-c; 7-b; 8-d; 9-g; 10-f

72 1-c; 2-e; 3-j; 4-f; 5-i; 6-b; 7-d; 8-k; 9-a; 10-g; 11-h; 12-l

73 1-e; 2-g; 3-d; 4-c; 5-a; 6-h; 7-i; 8-b; 9-f

74 1-g; 2-d; 3-k; 4-a; 5-i; 6-e; 7-c; 8-f; 9-h; 10-j; 11-b

75 1-F-d; 2-C-e; 3-I-g; 4-H-h; 5-A-f; 6-B-i; 7-G-b; 8-E-c; 9-D-a

76 1-d; 2-h; 3-j; 4-e; 5-k; 6-a; 7-f; 8-i; 9-c; 10-g; 11-b

77 1-f; 2-i; 3-g; 4-a; 5-e; 6-c; 7-k; 8-b; 9-h; 10-j; 11-d

78 1. false, we are not told; 2. true; 3. false, cattle are not mentioned; 4. false, the Wise Men were told to follow the star; 5. false, an angel not angels; 6. false, no number is given; 7. true; 8. true; 9. false, we are not told; 10. false, Herod wanted to kill him; 11. true

79 1-e; 2-g; 3-h; 4-i; 5-a; 6-f; 7-b; 8-d; 9-c

80 1-c; 2-g; 3-f; 4-e; 5-h; 6-i; 7-b; 8-j; 9-a; 10-d;

81 1-c; 2-h; 3-a; 4-k; 5-g; 6-b; 7-f; 8-j; 9-d; 10-1; 11-i; 12-e

82 1-e; 2-h; 3-i; 4-a; 5-j; 6-d; 7-k; 8-b; 9-g; 10-f; 11-c

83 1-i; 2-d; 3-h; 4-e; 5-f; 6-a; 7-b; 8-j; 9-g; 10-k; 11-c

84 1-c; 2-e; 3-i; 4-j; 5-a; 6-f; 7-h; 8-b; 9-g; 10-d

85 1-c; 2-i; 3-e; 4-h; 5-f; 6-b; 7-g; 8-a; 9-d; 10-j

86 1. Moses and Aaron; 2. John (the Baptist); 3. The Spirit of God; 4. Amos (God); 5. An Ethiopian eunuch; 6. Jesus; 7. Moses; 8. A sick man; 9. Elijah; 10. Noah

87 1-c; 2-j; 3-d; 4-e; 5-i; 6-f; 7-h; 8-b; 9-g; 10-a

88 1-j; 2-i; 3-a; 4-h; 5-b; 6-g; 7-c; 8-f; 9-d; 10-e

89 1-e; 2-i; 3-g; 4-b; 5-d; 6-h; 7-a; 8-f; 9-j; 10-c

90 1. Egyptians, Exodus 14:25; 2. Sisera's mother, Judges 5:28; 3. Ezekiel, Ezekiel 1:16; 4. Daniel, Daniel 7:1,9; 5. the enemies of God, Psalm 83:2,13; 6. Jeremiah, Jeremiah 18:3-6; 7. Solomon, 1 Kings 7:1,27-30; 8. Ezekiel, Ezekiel 10:6; 9. Nebuchadrezzar, Ezekiel 26:7-10; 10. Nineveh, Nahum 3:2,7

91 1. Exodus and Deuteronomy; 2. Psalms; 3. Proverbs; 4. Jonah; 5. Acts; 6. Joshua; 7. Esther; 8. Daniel; 9. Matthew; 10. Genesis; 11. Philemon

92 1. mountain; 2. Gethsemane; 3. desert; 4. tomb; 5. baptized; 6. Calvary; 7. teaching; 8. house; 9. upper room; 10. Judea

93 1-d; 2-h; 3-k; 4-a; 5-j; 6-b; 7-i; 8-f; 9-c; 10-g; 11-e
94 1. John the Baptist; 2. Jesus; 3. Joshua; 4. Job; 5. Solomon; 6. Peter; 7. Esther; 8. Samuel; 9. Samaritan woman; 10. Martha
95 1. Tamar; 2. Naomi; 3. Zeruah; 4. Anna; 5. She gave all she had; 6. Ruth; 7. He raised her dead son; 8. wise woman of Tekoah; 9. seven men were chosen to minister to the people; 10. Orpah
96 1. Philip; 2. Paul and Silas; 3. Stephen; 4. Paul; 5. Daniel; 6. Dorcas; 7. Andrew; 8. John the Baptist; 9. Matthias and Barsabas; 10. Peter; 11. Philip; 12. Barnabas and Saul; 23. Priscilla and Aquila
97 1. Abigail's; 2. Sarah; 3. Dinah; 4. Julia; 5. queen of Sheba; 6. Huldah; 7. Herodias; 8. Mary; 9. Elisabeth; 10. Rahab's; 11. Esther
98 1-d; 2-f; 3-e; 4-j; 5-i; 6-c; 7-b; 8-g; 9-h; 10-a
99 1. shittim; 2. cedar; 3. cedar; 4. olive; 5. fir; 6. fir, cedar; 7. oak; 8. fir; 9. olive, pine, myrtle, palm; 10. shittim; 11. gopher; 12. cedar
100 1-7; 2-12; 3-40; 4-969; 5-100; 6-18; 7-90; 8-12; 9-10; 10-40; 11-3½ ; 12-2; 13-500